ROY BLATCHFORD

THE TEACHERS' STANDARDS IN THE CLASSROOM

FOURTH EDITION

Learning Matters
A SAGE Publishing Company
1 Oliver's Yard
55 City Road
London EC1Y 1SP

SAGE Publications Inc.
2455 Teller Road
Thousand Oaks, California 91320

SAGE Publications India Pvt Ltd
B 1/I 1 Mohan Cooperative Industrial Area
Mathura Road
New Delhi 110 044

SAGE Publications Asia-Pacific Pte Ltd
3 Church Street
#10-04 Samsung Hub
Singapore 049483

© 2021 Roy Blatchford

First published in 2013 by SAGE/Learning Matters
Second edition 2015
Third edition 2017
Third edition updates completed by David Waugh
Fourth edition 2021
Fourth edition updates completed by Deborah
Wilkinson and James Martin

Editor: Amy Thornton
Senior project editor: Chris Marke
Project management: Deer Park Productions
Marketing manager: Lorna Patkai
Cover design: Wendy Scott
Typeset by: C&M Digitals (P) Ltd, Chennai, India
Printed in the UK

Library of Congress Control Number: 2020942873

British Library Cataloguing in Publication Data

A catalogue record for this book is available
from the British Library

ISBN 978-1-5297-2525-4
ISBN 978-1-5297-2524-7 (pbk)

At SAGE we take sustainability seriously. Most of our products are printed in the UK using responsibly sourced
papers and boards. When we print overseas we ensure sustainable papers are used as measured by the
PREPS grading system. We undertake an annual audit to monitor our sustainability.

CONTENTS

ACKNOWLEDGEMENTS

UPDATES TO THE FOURTH EDITION

Updates for the fourth edition were completed by Deborah Wilkinson and James Martin.

Dr Deborah Wilkinson is a qualified primary teacher with over 20 years' experience in education. She is currently a Senior Lecturer in Education at the University of Chichester, where she teaches outdoor learning, primary science and STEM. She is interested in how questions are used in primary science lessons and how collaborative action research can support changes in teaching practice.

James Martin is a qualified primary school teacher with over 25 years' experience in education. He is Head of School Partnership at the University of Chichester, where he also teaches professional studies in the role of the teacher and the needs of the learner. James also has experience of training teachers internationally. He spent two summers (2018 and 2019) training 300 teachers in Beijing.

ABOUT THE AUTHOR

Roy Blatchford CBE is Founding Director of the National Education Trust in the UK, an independent foundation which leads excellent practice and innovation in education.

Previously he served as one of Her Majesty's Inspector of Schools (HMI) in England, with national responsibilities for school improvement and for the inspection of outstanding schools. Roy has extensive experience of writing inspection frameworks, nationally and internationally, and has inspected and reviewed over 1,000 schools and colleges in Europe, USA, Middle East and India.

Roy was Principal of Walton High and Walton Learning Centre in Milton Keynes, opened in September 1999 and described by the inspectorate as 'a first class centre of learning – innovative and inspiring'. He was Founding Director (1996-8) of Reading Is Fundamental, UK, a non-profit organisation developing children's reading and family literacy. From 1986-96 he was headteacher of an Oxfordshire comprehensive school serving 1200+ 11-19-year-old students. He spent his early teaching career in inner-London schools, youth and adult services.

For 30 years Roy has been an international trainer and speaker on English and literacy, school improvement, leadership and innovation. He was Visiting Professor in English, Rollins College, Florida. He has served as an adviser to various UK governments, including Deputy Chair of the DfE Teachers' Standards Review (2012) and of the Headteachers' Standards Review (2014).

Roy has worked with HM Prison Service, the NHS and the Arts Council in a number of voluntary capacities, and is a Visiting Fellow at Oxford Brookes University. He is co-founder of the Mumbai-based education foundation Adhyayan.

He is the author/editor of over 150 books. Recent titles include *Sparkling Classrooms, The Restless School, A Guide to the Headteachers' Standards, Self-Improving Schools: The Journey to Excellence, The Three Minute Leader, The Forgotten Third*. His BBC Radio programme *Government versus the Teachers*, commissioned to mark the 70th anniversary of the 1944 Education Act, was broadcast to acclaim in March 2014.

He was appointed **CBE** for services to education in the 2016 New Year Honours.

PREFACE

10,000 HOURS – WHAT MAKES A GREAT TEACHER?

Thomas More: Why not be a teacher? You'd be a fine teacher, perhaps a great one.

Richard Rich: If I was, who would know it?

Thomas More: You, your pupils, your friends, God. Not a bad public, that.

(A Man for All Seasons)

What makes anyone accomplished at anything? Influential psychologist Anders Ericsson and polemicist Malcolm Gladwell tell us that 10,000 hours of *purposeful practice* are necessary to create real proficiency – and maybe the platform for stand-out excellence.

Think of The Silver Beatles playing the clubs of Hamburg; Lewis Hamilton, aged six, driving go-karts; the young Venus Williams on Palm Beach tennis courts; Bill Gates or Steve Jobs in their formative 'garage years' – each driven by different motives, investing hours and hours to perfect what later became their greatness.

Take a regular classroom teacher, teaching 1,000 lessons a year. That's 10,000 in a decade. At a careful estimate, over several decades I have taught about 30,000 sessions to learners of all ages. And in various guises, I have been an 'observer' in just over 15,000 classrooms during the past fifteen years.

What do I experience when I am in the presence of an accomplished teacher, irrespective of context and location: from Newcastle to New York, Geneva to Pune, Riyadh to Kuala Belait? Reflecting on vivid examples, I identify ten prevalent features in the cocktail, variously distilled.

1. **Knowledge.** No teacher can survive without the fount of knowledge which lies at the core of their everyday practice. Good teachers have an innate generosity to want to share what they know. For the skilled early years' practitioner that knowledge lies in a deep understanding of how young children grow, and how best to intervene or draw back when children are developing their independent learning habits. For the teacher of an International Baccalaureate (IB) French class studying Albert Camus, it is the teacher's facility to cross-reference Sartre, Gide or Heidegger to open up an appreciation of existentialism. *The skilled teacher has knowledge effortlessly rising out of them like sap from a tree – and keeps practising.*

2. **Craft.** In many walks of life a 'craftsman' is revered for her or his well-honed skills, whether cooking, sculpting or operating medically. The craft of the classroom involves its own special blend: skilled configuration of the classroom and management of pupils, time creatively orchestrated, 'less is more' lesson planning, judicious harnessing of resources, intelligent questioning and thoughtful feedback, that balance of critique and worthy praise, wise promotion of mastery, scholarship and enquiry. *The reflective practitioner commands the classroom, physically and intellectually.*

3. **Passion.** A love of being in a classroom with pupils is a prerequisite for accomplished teachers, joyfully sharing those personal and professional passions which first drew them to work in schools. To watch an enthusiastic, knowledgeable teacher embed through song and repetition an understanding of key letters and sounds in a Year 1 class is to witness enviable practice. Equally impressive is the Year 9 PE teacher, a skilled sportswoman in her own right, enabling 'sport for all and excellence for some' in a lesson on badminton forehand and backhand serves. *The passion for excellence, rooted in the teacher's own achievements, is palpable and often thrilling.*

4. **Values.** In a teacher's every utterance and body language their values about education and schooling shine through. Values reflect our sense of right and wrong and what we believe to be important to us in life. Join a teacher who is reading *The Boy in the Striped Pyjamas* with their Year 6 class; see how adroitly they field the most challenging of questions and how they support those pupils struggling emotionally with the novel's content. Or be party to an A-level history seminar wrestling with the difference between freedom fighters and terrorists, where the teacher harnesses his considerable knowledge of Gandhi, Mandela and Guevara to present objective evidence upon which students can make a judgement. *A teacher's unambiguous set of values, embodying integrity and clear conscience, underpin memorable classroom practice.*

5. **Fun.** Teaching is all about communicating to students that great double act: the fun and fundamentals of learning. Watch a gifted teacher of mathematics – with a basket of home-made, practical resources – play around with prime numbers in a

Year 5 class, or that same teacher work with his non-specialist colleagues to enable them to plan confidently a session for Year 4 pupils on the Fibonacci Sequence: 0, 1, 1, 2, 3, 5, 8, 13, 21, 34 ... Dealing in fun enables students of any age to feel confident about making mistakes, learning from them and achieving that 'aha' moment of breakthrough comprehension. The fundamentals in any subject demand practice, memorisation, repetition. *The fun in learning is about teachers and students sharing humour and wit; fun is equally rooted in risk-taking and digression.*

6. **Creativity.** The imaginative, thinking out-of-the-box spirit lies deep in great teachers' hearts and minds. They positively embrace digression and those unplanned moments of epiphany for their students. Focus on a group of Year 8 students doing a fair test in science, when the teacher comes along and introduces a rogue substance to create intellectual confusion. Listen carefully to an English as an additional language (EAL) teacher with a group of Year 10 boys newly arrived from Serbia, harnessing Google Translate to explore the language of mathematical shapes. Creativity is an element equally at home in physics, geography or drama. *The creative teacher has a predictable unpredictability about their person.*

7. **Expectations.** Show me a fine teacher who does not have the highest expectations of those they teach, wherever and whomever they are teaching. When record-breakers in any walk of life achieve a new record, their starting point is an unshakeable belief that they *can* do it. The skilled teacher knows authoritatively their pupils and can cajole, enthuse, provoke, extend as they judge: we might employ the term 'differentiation' here. Observe a passionate teacher of English enable *every* Year 7 student to grasp the metaphors in Ted Hughes's 'The Thought Fox'; see that teacher do the same for *every* Year 11 student in her class, climbing inside the complex imagery in Sylvia Plath's 'The Bell Jar'. *What teachers expect is what they get in any classroom, in any subject and in any context.*

8. **Empathy.** The ability to 'climb inside the learner's skin' is a hallmark of those teachers who live long in their pupils' memories. Great biology teachers may well have an encyclopaedic knowledge of how an *E. coli* bacterium performs differently from a sub-atomic particle when observed in a laboratory. The GCSE students are perplexed, and remain so even after the second explanation – until the teacher thinks differently and tries a third explanation which approaches the problem from the learner's less experienced viewpoint. Breakthrough in understanding comes. Students of any age testify to the fact that experienced teachers can empathise with the learner's predicament, can 'connect' emotionally with them, can see that grey sometimes has its place alongside black and white. *Empathy is that vital capacity in a teacher to imagine and understand that the learner may well have a different frame of reference.*

9. **Resilience.** Building learners' resilience in a contemporary world of 'snow-plough' learning devices is not to be underestimated: 'What's a cosine?' asks the teacher.

'It's that button on the calculator,' comes the flawless answer. As vital as leading lessons with fun is the teacher's commitment to lead with intrigue: taking pupils out of their comfort zones, making learning difficult and perplexing as the moment arises. What doesn't kill you intellectually certainly makes you stronger – ask any student of further maths. The wise and practised teacher also recognises that their own trade is a demanding one: knowing how to pace oneself daily, weekly, termly is an art and a science in itself. *Resilience is two track: one for the pupils' stamina in new learning and one for the teachers' self-preservation and ultimate flourishing. Live to teach another day.*

10. **X factor.** The cocktail is more or less prepared but the distillation is incomplete without the X factor. No two teachers are the same – they may embody in many ways the nine aspects outlined above. Yet the unashamed joy of the generous teacher is that their own commanding classroom practice is, in the end, a matter of individual taste, tact and style. Each teacher has their own X factor, their unique ingredient of the pedagogical potion. *Classroom excellence becomes their habit and their 'public' never forget the magic.*

WHO IS THIS BOOK FOR, HOW IS IT ORGANISED AND HOW CAN IT BE USED?

The Teachers' Standards in the Classroom is aimed primarily at those training to teach, in whatever setting. Just as the Standards themselves are addressed to classrooms in primary, special and secondary schools, so is the intent of this book. Whether you are training to teach early years' children, lower secondary pupils or sixth-form students, the book should offer something by way of information, reflection, advice and inspiration.

Equally, it is intended that the content will be relevant to teachers who are already qualified and experienced, and who are seeking to refresh their own professional development in the light of what will for them be newly expressed standards and expectations.

Teaching is quite simply one of the best jobs in the world, for the many, many who enjoy it. For that small minority of teachers - and sadly you meet a few in staffrooms - who do not enjoy their work or have become tired of its challenges, teaching must be a sad existence, for them and, worryingly, for those they teach. It is a profession to be embraced with both hands, positive spirit, good health, a lively mind and an unequivocal commitment to young people.

The book follows a straightforward format.

There is an introduction and background section, which gives a context for the Teachers' Standards which first became effective from 1 September 2012. This section concludes with a discussion of the Preamble to the actual Standards, a statement of professional intent and aspiration for all teachers to embrace.

Chapters 1 to 8 consider in turn each of the eight key Standards – Part 1 of the Teachers' Standards document – as set out by the Department for Education (DfE), examining their content and purpose, and how trainee teachers might be expected to demonstrate, with evidence, that they are meeting the Standards. For those in training settings around the country, whether school or higher education based, the text seeks to complement the expert guidance afforded by tutors and their own supporting materials.

Chapter 9 focuses on Part 2 of the Standards, unambiguously titled 'Personal and Professional Conduct', and applicable to all who teach in the nation's schools, whatever their position or length of service within the teaching profession.

Chapter 10 is entitled 'Master Teacher'. Why? In establishing the Teachers' Standards, the DfE invited the group writing the Standards to create a further set of draft criteria describing what might be the qualities and distinguishing features of high-performing teachers. This Master Teacher Standard is included here by way of 'extension material' for interested readers and may have particular resonance for experienced teachers within the profession.

Chapter 11 presents important detail from the Ofsted *School Inspection Handbook* (Ofsted, 2019a), and how Ofsted inspectors judge the quality of teaching and learning in classrooms. Further, it examines how the Teachers' Standards and the Ofsted criteria compare.

Chapter 12 extends readers' understanding of the evidence which is to be found in the annual report of the Chief Inspector of Schools, highlighting key aspects of less and more effective classroom practices as observed nationally.

Chapter 13 gives trainee and other teachers the opportunity to reflect on their practice in a range of curriculum areas, coming to a view as to whether what they are doing meets, with clear evidence, a number of the Teachers' Standards. A selection of 'best practice' checklists are featured here.

Chapter 14 presents a wider perspective on successful schools. Fulfilled and confident teachers deserve to be well led by those who believe in an aspirational culture and to work in schools which are both restless to improve and consistently outward facing.

And there are four 'Interludes' which punctuate the book. Each of these is presented as a series of questions to ask yourself when entering classrooms across the 3-18 age range in search of good and excellent practice. They are rooted in the author's own observations of more than 10,000 lessons in schools and settings around the world over the past decade. The more experienced you become in classrooms, the more you will discover that you are able to ask these questions intuitively.

Finally, a few house style points.

- As formally set out by the DfE, each of the Teachers' Standards has its own heading, followed by a number of bulleted subheadings. The bullets, which are an integral part of the Standards, are designed to *amplify the scope of each heading.* For ease of reference in this book, the bullets have been identified by letters, from A to E. Good teaching, by its very nature, is a distinctive cocktail of skills and techniques, so readers will inevitably find some subheadings across the Standards complementing and reinforcing one another.

- To help the reader interrogate the Standards and other parts of the book, analysis and advice are presented under three headings:

   o *Commentary* – offers pointers as to how teachers may interpret the Standards in their everyday practice.

   o *Reflections* – seek to develop the good habits of the 'reflective practitioner'; these could be used as starters for group discussion in a training context.

   o *Evidence* – for the trainee teacher, suggestions about providing evidence against the Standards to a tutor mentor, whether they are visiting the trainee in the classroom or viewing an online portfolio, or during a group session at the training institution.

- The term 'classroom' has been used throughout the book. It is used in the generic sense, to include workshops, laboratories, gymnasia, sports fields and outdoor settings, dance studios, music practice rooms and any space where teachers may find themselves leading young minds.

- The word 'pupils' is taken to include children, learners, students, whatever the reader's preferred term might be, given his or her individual teaching setting.

- When referring to an individual teacher or pupil, licence has sometimes been taken with accompanying singulars and plurals; for example, the grammatically incorrect 'they' is used rather than the potentially clumsy 'he/she'. This goes against my purist instincts, but is a stylistic imperfection which I hope the reader can live with in this context.

Roy Blatchford
Oxford 2020

INTRODUCTION TO THE TEACHERS' STANDARDS

BACKGROUND

September 2012 saw the introduction of new Teachers' Standards which replaced the existing qualified teacher status (QTS) and Core Standards, and the Code of Practice for Registered Teachers in England from the General Teaching Council for England (GTCE). The new Standards set out the minimum requirements for teachers' professional practice and conduct. Teachers' performance is to be assessed against them as part of the appraisal arrangements for schools.

In drawing up the standards during 2011, the Independent Review of Teachers' Standards was given the remit to develop new standards of competence, ethics and behaviour which reflect the trust and professionalism society should expect from its teachers (DfE, 2011a). To that end, the new Standards begin with a Preamble, a founding statement of expectations:

Teachers make the education of their pupils their first concern, and are accountable for achieving the highest possible standards in work and conduct. Teachers act with honesty and integrity, have strong subject knowledge, keep their knowledge and skills as teachers up-to-date and are self-critical, forge positive professional relationships, and work with parents in the best interests of their pupils.

(DfE, 2012a, p7)

WHAT HAPPENS IN CLASSROOMS?

On a personal note, I have had the great privilege during the past decade to observe over 10,000 classrooms, from Mumbai to New York, Barcelona to Birmingham, Jeddah to Jarrow. At their best, these are the vibrant classrooms which teachers create because they are spending many of their waking hours within them. They are the places where young minds flourish. These sparkling classrooms are places and atmospheres which remain long in the minds and spirits of the learners.

When I joined Her Majesty's Inspectorate (HMI) in 2004, David Bell HMCI advised me to reflect on the wisdom of a previous chief inspector, Martin Roseveare: *You should remember that when you visit a school it is an everyday affair for you, but an unusual and important occasion for the school.* I remind myself of those words every day I sign in to a school's visitors' book.

In the academic year 2013-14 I observed over 700 lessons as part of the National Education Trust's school improvement services (**www.nationaleducationtrust.net**). Special, primary, secondary, state and independent, home and abroad - schools have welcomed me with warm hospitality and in the spirit of championing what is great, recognising what is good and suggesting a few even-better-ifs.

What did I learn during that year in classrooms?

- That childhood is safe in the nation's primary schools.

- That in socially challenging schools the teachers have to run just for the pupils to stand still.

- That great lessons are all about richness of task, rooted in teachers' excellent subject knowledge and passion to share that knowledge with students.

- That pupils' prior knowledge of a subject is endlessly surprising.

- That in the best classrooms IT is a useful tool for teaching and learning when used appropriately, like a pair of scissors - no more no less.

- That skilled early years' practitioners have much to teach everyone else about the power of timely digression and intervention.

- That teachers spend hours marking, but too often pupils don't do justice to that marking.

- That doing more of the same is not going to transform standards of attainment - doing *differently* can.

- That teachers may cry when you tell them they have taught a great lesson.

- That the best teachers are children at heart.

- That sitting in the best lessons, you just don't want to leave ...

In the best schools I visit there is a central paradox which runs through them like Brighton through a stick of rock. It is this: the schools are at one and the same time very secure in their values and ways of doing yet simultaneously restless to improve.

So too with the sparkling classroom practitioner who is absolutely in the grip of well-tried, tested and effective practices yet simultaneously questing to improve their teaching of a particular topic or skill. The best teachers ask at the end of a day: what have I learned as a teacher today? What shall I do (a) the same and (b) differently next time?

WHAT THE TEACHERS' STANDARDS SAY

The Review considered a wide range of international and national evidence, including evidence submitted by key users of standards, before developing the Teachers' Standards. The new Standards had to provide a benchmark of the minimum requirements that should be expected of trainees and teachers.

In essence, the Standards had to raise the bar and highlight the characteristics of good teaching. Above all, the Standards needed to be clear, simple and assessable, and identify the key elements of teaching and the expectations of professional conduct that underpin the practice of teachers at all career stages.

The Review was clear, however, that the Standards should not define the award of QTS and the end of a teacher's induction period as two separate career stages, principally because the induction period should be about consolidating initial teacher training (ITT) and demonstrating consistency of practice. Trainees and teachers should demonstrate that they meet all of the Standards, which define the level of practice at which all qualified teachers should be expected to perform.

The Standards do not prescribe in detail what good or outstanding teaching looks like; this should be determined by ITT providers, headteachers and teachers, using their professional judgement as relevant to context, roles and responsibilities. The Standards should assist them in making such decisions by providing a clear framework within which such judgements can be made.

The Review also recommended that the Post-Threshold, Excellent Teacher and Advanced Skills Teacher standards should be discontinued, and advocated the introduction of a Master Teacher Standard (see Chapter 10 and DfE, 2011b). This Standard is made up of five core domains (modelled on international best practice) within which very good teachers can demonstrate their abilities:

1. Knowledge

2. Classroom Performance

3. Outcomes

4. Environment and Ethos

5. Professional Context

It was the Review Group's view that the Teachers' Standards, and the proposed Master Teacher Standard, would provide a new progressive career framework for teachers to both raise the prestige of the profession and improve teacher quality.

From my personal standpoint as one of the lead authors, the Teachers' Standards are a once-in-a-generation opportunity for teachers across the country to unite behind a set of professional expectations which are focused unequivocally on the classroom. If all teachers meet these expectations, we shall have a profession of which society can be rightly proud.

KEY QUOTATIONS FROM THE TEACHERS' STANDARDS DOCUMENT

The Teachers' Standards are published in a self-contained eight-page document which should be read by all teachers (DfE, 2012a). The following list of key quotations is particularly relevant to trainee teachers. The source of each quotation is indicated.

> *The new standards will apply to the vast majority of teachers regardless of their career stage. The Teachers' Standards will apply to: trainees working towards QTS; all teachers completing their statutory induction period; and those covered by the new performance appraisal arrangements.*

> **(para 3, p2)**

> *The new standards define the minimum level of practice expected of trainees and teachers from the point of being awarded QTS.*

> **(para 5, p2)**

> *The new standards will need to be applied as appropriate to the role and context within which a trainee or teacher is practising. Providers of initial teacher training (ITT) will assess trainees against the standards in a way that is consistent with what could reasonably be expected of a trainee teacher prior to the award of QTS.*

> **(para 6, p3)**

> *Headteachers (or appraisers) will assess qualified teachers against the standards to a level that is consistent with what should reasonably be expected of a teacher in the relevant role and at the relevant stage of their career.*

> **(para 7, p3)**

The new standards are presented as separate headings, numbered 1 to 8, each of which is accompanied by a number of bulleted subheadings. The bullets, which are an integral part of the standards, are designed to amplify the scope of each heading.

(para 13, p4)

The bulleted subheadings should not be interpreted as separate standards in their own right, but should be used by those assessing trainees and teachers to track progress against the standard, to determine areas where additional development might need to be observed, or to identify areas where a trainee or teacher is already demonstrating excellent practice to that standard.

(para 13, p4)

Appropriate self-evaluation, reflection and professional development activity is critical to improving teachers' practice at all career stages. The standards set out clearly the key areas in which a teacher should be able to assess his or her own practice and receive feedback from colleagues.

(para 14, p4)

As their careers progress, teachers will be expected to extend the depth and breadth of knowledge, skill and understanding that they demonstrate in meeting the standards, as is judged appropriate to the role they are fulfilling and the context in which they are working.

(para 14, p4)

REFLECTIONS

1. Make sure you have a clear understanding of these key quotations, and how they apply to your first year in teaching.

2. What record-keeping are you developing to ensure you are:

   - tracking progress against the Standards
   - determining areas for development
   - identifying your best practice?

3. What systems are securely in place to ensure you have prompt and timely feedback on all aspects of your developing practice?

4. Are you clear about the 'sign-off' procedures relating to your meeting of the Standards?

THE PREAMBLE TO THE STANDARDS

Preamble

Teachers make the education of their pupils their first concern and are accountable for achieving the highest possible standards in work and conduct. Teachers act with honesty and integrity, have strong subject knowledge, keep their knowledge and skills as teachers up-to-date and are self-critical, forge positive professional relationships and work with parents in the best interests of their pupils.

(DfE, 2012a, p7)

The Preamble summarises the values and behaviour that all teachers must demonstrate throughout their careers. At one level it is perhaps a statement of the obvious, and such a description has not previously been applied to the teaching profession in this country.

Yet preambles such as this are no stranger to other professions. They have long been an integral part of conditions of service for doctors, lawyers, accountants, architects and others.

By way of comparison, the reader may be interested to glance over the following, drawn from different professions, and reflect on the various expectations which are set down, for the trainee and the experienced professional alike.

Lawyers

In a society founded on respect for the rule of law the lawyer fulfils a special role. His duties do not begin and end with the faithful performance of what he is instructed to do so far as the law permits. A lawyer must serve the interests of justice as well as those whose rights and liberties he is trusted to assert and defend, and it is his duty not only to plead his client's cause but to be his adviser.

A lawyer's function therefore lays on him a variety of legal and moral obligations (sometimes appearing to be in conflict with each other) towards:

- *the client;*

- *the courts and other authorities before whom the lawyer pleads his client's cause or acts on his behalf;*

- *the legal profession in general and each fellow member of it in particular;*

- *the public for whom the existence of a free and independent profession, bound together by respect for rules made by the profession itself, is an essential means of safeguarding human rights in face of the power of the state and other interests in society.*

(From the European Lawyers Code of Conduct, www.barstandardsboard.org.uk)

Architects

You are expected at all times to act with honesty and integrity and to avoid any actions or situations which are inconsistent with your professional obligations. This standard underpins the Code and will be taken to be required in any consideration of your conduct under any of the other standards.

You should not make any statement which is contrary to your professional opinion or which you know to be misleading, unfair to others or discreditable to the profession.

Where a conflict of interest arises you are expected to disclose it in writing and manage it to the satisfaction of all affected parties. You should seek written confirmation that all parties involved give their informed consent to your continuing to act. Where this consent is not received you should cease acting for one or more of the parties.

Where you make or receive any payment or other inducement for the introduction or referral of work, you should disclose the arrangement to the client or prospective client at the outset.

(From the Architects Registration Board code of conduct, www.arb.org.uk/professional_standards)

Doctors

Patients need good doctors. Good doctors make the care of their patients their first concern: they are competent, keep their knowledge and skills up to date, establish and maintain good relationships with patients and colleagues, are honest and trustworthy, and act with integrity.

(From *Good Medical Practice*, General Medical Council, 2012, www.gmc-uk.org/guidance/good_medical_practice)

REFLECTIONS

1. In what ways are the above similar and different in their expectations and values?
2. How do they compare in content with the Preamble to the Teachers' Standards?
3. Is there anything you would amend about the Preamble to the Teachers' Standards?

1

SET HIGH EXPECTATIONS WHICH INSPIRE, MOTIVATE AND CHALLENGE PUPILS

1   **A teacher must: set high expectations which inspire, motivate and challenge pupils**

   A   establish a safe and stimulating environment for pupils, rooted in mutual respect

   B   set goals that stretch and challenge pupils of all backgrounds, abilities and dispositions

   C   demonstrate consistently the positive attitudes, values and behaviour which are expected of pupils.

(DfE, 2012a, p7)

—————— COMMENTARY ——————

The cornerstone of effective teaching lies in the expectations teachers set down for their pupils. Hence the Teachers' Standards begin – in Standard 1 – with expecting all teachers to set high expectations which inspire, motivate and challenge pupils. All three verbs are equally important, though each of them will

(Continued)

(Continued)

quite properly be interpreted differently by the teacher of a Reception class or an A-level economics group.

In amplifying the scope of the Standard 1 heading, there are three stated areas for teachers to focus upon.

A   Safety is non-negotiable, and this will take on a different dimension if the teacher is at work on a school playing field, in a drama studio or in a science laboratory. The environment itself needs to stimulate the learner, and that may be through wall displays or the exhibiting of artefacts relevant to the subject being studied. And the whole culture of the classroom must of course promote a learning climate within which pupils and adults treat one another with dignity and where mutual respect is of the essence.

B   By their very nature, all classrooms contain a population of unique individuals, including the teacher and any support staff. The teacher must set significant store by, and invest time in, getting to know those they teach. Not only do pupils come from different family backgrounds, creeds and cultures, but abilities and dispositions vary, often significantly, as do aspirations and pupils' own self-esteem. Once teachers know the distinctive characteristics and characters of the pupils, they are then in a strong position to ensure that lessons are planned and delivered in a way that ensures all pupils are challenged and stretched.

C   Pupils will always mirror their teachers' attitudes and behaviour. This is as true of seven-year-olds in an infant classroom as it is of a GCSE class of teenagers. Where a teacher is negative and indulges in the 'dark sarcasm of the classroom', pupils will surely be infected by such an approach. Where a teacher is consistently upbeat and positive, the class will catch the same mood. The teacher's positive values, warmly shared, complemented by their own modelling of good behaviours, have a decisive impact on the well-being and fruitful commerce of the classroom.

REFLECTIONS

1.   Think of a classroom you have visited which immediately grabbed your attention and evoked a very positive emotional response. What were the features of the physical organisation and 'feel' which caught your attention?

2.   Think of a classroom you have visited which gave out the opposite impressions. What were its features?

3. Which techniques have you observed among experienced teachers for getting to know pupils quickly and intelligently?

4. Think of a lesson you have seen where the teacher was clearly able to challenge the intellectual thinking of all pupils. How did they do this effectively?

5. From observing fellow professionals, we learn what *not* to do as well as what to do. Reflect on the everyday classroom practice of a teacher you have seen whose values and positive classroom behaviours you would wish to emulate.

EVIDENCE

Demonstrate evidence to your tutor/mentor of:

*   a safe and welcoming physical environment;
*   stimulating subject-related displays of pupils' work;
*   your strong knowledge of each pupil's abilities and dispositions;
*   high expectations permeating classroom practice;
*   your positive verbal and body language towards the pupils;
*   a clear set of shared values, rooted in mutual respect.

EXAMPLE OF GOOD PRACTICE

Working with pupils to devise rules for the classroom

Kirsty, an NQT whose first class was a Y3 group which had a reputation for disruptive behaviour in KS1, discussed strategies for creating a positive learning environment with her new and more experienced colleagues. She decided to work with the children on the first day of term to devise a set of simple class rules. Kirsty encouraged children to discuss the kind of classroom and behaviour they would like and then, using shared and independent writing, eight rules were developed. Kirsty typed these and produced attractive posters as well as individual cards for children. She then referred to the rules and asked children to look at them when there were infractions.

During her first observations from teaching colleagues, staff commented on the calm and productive atmosphere in the classroom, as well as children's appreciation of what constituted good working behaviour and what did not.

STANDARD 1: SET HIGH EXPECTATIONS WHICH INSPIRE, MOTIVATE AND CHALLENGE PUPILS

Have I met Standard 1?

- I have communicated and promoted positive attitudes, values and behaviour by personal example.

- I have encouraged learners to contribute views, and to reflect on, evaluate and learn from their mistakes.

- I have implemented the school's policies on equality, discipline, bullying and harassment, safeguarding and child protection.

- I have established high expectations for learner behaviour, and resolved conflicts inside and outside the classroom appropriately.

- I have planned work at a suitably high level in relation to age and ability and to external benchmarks such as national curriculum level descriptors.

- I have planned to meet diverse needs and demonstrated an understanding of the needs of minority groups.

2

PROMOTE GOOD PROGRESS AND OUTCOMES BY PUPILS

2 A teacher must: promote good progress and outcomes by pupils

A   be accountable for pupils' attainment, progress and outcomes

B   be aware of pupils' capabilities and prior knowledge and plan teaching to build on these

C   guide pupils to reflect on the progress they have made and their emerging needs

D   demonstrate knowledge and understanding of how pupils learn and how this impacts on teaching

E   encourage pupils to take a responsible and conscientious attitude to their own work and study.

(DfE, 2012a, p7)

────────── **COMMENTARY** ──────────

Schools exist first and foremost to serve the educational needs of their pupils. Rightly, schools are judged by parents and the wider community on their track record

(Continued)

(Continued)

in (a) how pupils make progress in their various subjects, and (b) the final examination grades and other awards they achieve. It is also fair to say that society at large judges the wider school system on how well it is preparing the next generation of healthy, active and participating citizens.

Standard 2 shines a proper spotlight on the expectation that all pupils should make good progress and enjoy good outcomes during their compulsory school years.

In amplifying the scope of the Standard 2 heading, there are five stated areas for teachers to focus upon.

A   The lead adjective here is accountable. As professionals, teachers are fundamentally accountable for what happens in their classrooms. They are accountable to the pupils they teach, to the parents of those pupils and, usually through line management systems, to the leadership of the school. *What* are teachers accountable for? First on the list is what a pupil attains, that is academic attainment as measured by tests and examinations. Today's teacher must have a sure command of the school's and pupils' performance data. Second, there is the academic progress a pupil makes over time with the teacher. Third, there are the broader outcomes which, depending on setting, may be measured through aspects of social, emotional and physical development.

B   Standard 1 highlights the vital importance of a teacher knowing the abilities and dispositions of pupils in their class. Building on this base, teachers will come to identify individual pupils' capabilities. Critically, it is vital to identify also what prior knowledge of a subject or skill a pupil already possesses. Failure to do this means pupils will make limited progress. Once armed with a thorough knowledge of all the pupils in a classroom, effective lesson planning and the harnessing of suitable resources can take place.

C   Teaching and learning are a great double act. One requires the other. The effective teacher helps pupils, through various techniques, to think about the progress they are making, daily, weekly and over a term or a year. The teacher and pupil reflecting on progress together, through marking and dialogue, identify the next steps in learning and what particular support or extension might be required to ensure the pupil's individual needs are met. This is as true of an infant teacher observing the development of fine motor skills as it is of the GCSE history teacher concentrating on improving essay writing skills with their group.

D   In the same way that a hand surgeon needs to have detailed knowledge of the nerves, tendons and arteries of that part of the body, so the professional teacher needs excellent technical background know-how. The primary specialist will have a clear understanding of cognitive development in, say, seven-year-olds, and how teaching approaches need to be adjusted to secure effective progress in mathematics in a Year 2 classroom. Equally, the A-level teacher of economics will bring to seminar groups a secure command of the impact of different study skills and analytics, so that pupils can be helped to approach a demanding concept from different directions in order to grasp its complexities.

E   Skilful teaching is also about a degree of 'letting go'. The teacher cannot do it all. Consistent with the age and growing maturity of the pupil, the teacher should encourage independence. This independence will be demonstrated by pupils taking a responsible and conscientious approach to their classwork and homework. It will not happen by magic. Effective teachers nudge, cajole and model independent learning habits. Good teachers and good parents have in common that they give 'roots and wings' to their children.

REFLECTIONS

1.   What do you understand by the word 'accountable'? In your particular school setting, what lines of accountability are (a) clearly and (b) less clearly set out?

2.   Are you clear as to whom you are accountable and for what?

3.   How does the school in which you work define 'attainment', 'progress' and 'outcomes'? What is your working understanding of these terms?

4.   What is your command and working knowledge of (a) the whole school's data and (b) the performance data for the pupils you teach?

5.   What techniques do you plan to use to ensure that you have a good grasp of pupils' prior knowledge and capabilities?

6.   What have you observed by way of best practice in relation to teachers helping pupils reflect on progress?

7.   What particular strengths, knowledge and skills do you have which will enable you to gain a quick understanding of how pupils are learning in your classroom?

8.   Think of a teacher from your own school days who helped you become an independent learner. What 'tricks' did they use? How will you successfully promote responsible attitudes to work among the pupils you teach? How might you approach the pupil who is resistant to taking responsibility for his or her own learning?

EVIDENCE

Demonstrate evidence to your tutor/mentor of:

- pupils' attainment in one or two aspects of their learning;
- pupils' progress in another two aspects of learning;
- pupils' outcomes in social, physical or emotional development;
- lesson plans which reflect your strong analysis of pupils' prior knowledge;
- techniques you have used (a) to help pupils reflect on their own progress and (b) to encourage pupils to take responsibility for their own study;
- clear understanding of how pupils are learning effectively in your classroom and ways in which you have adjusted your teaching to better suit pupils' learning dispositions.

EXAMPLE OF GOOD PRACTICE

Developing writing

Faizal's Y11 history set included several pupils who found it difficult to produce the kind of writing which would be needed to gain them good marks in their forthcoming exams. He decided that he would model writing and use a writing sequence similar to one he had seen at a recent professional development course.

Faizal asked pupils to answer a series of questions about one of the topics they had covered and then made notes at the side of the board of key words and phrases. Most students were quite knowledgeable about the topic, if reluctant to write independently.

He then modelled the writing process by constructing an opening sentence and thinking aloud as he did so. When the pupils worked independently, he encouraged them to stop occasionally for paired reflection so that they could evaluate each other's work and suggest ways in which it might be improved. He emphasised the qualities which the writing would need in order to gain a good mark and asked pupils to focus on these. They were also encouraged to 'magpie' ideas from each other with Faizal making the point that they were not competing against each other and the objective was to enable everyone to produce better quality work as they prepared to work independently in their exams.

The lesson concluded with discussion and feedback and a reiteration of the key qualities needed for a good exam result.

STANDARD 2: PROMOTE GOOD PROGRESS AND OUTCOMES BY PUPILS

Have I met Standard 2?

- I have set realistic targets for learners, and involved them fully in every aspect of learning.

- I have monitored individual responses and used discussion and questioning to provide challenges at a variety of levels.

- I have demonstrated how I have modified my lesson planning in the light of my evaluations of impact.

- I have demonstrated how to use pupil-level and school-level data to gauge the impact of my teaching.

- I have successfully used feedback to and dialogue with individuals and groups in supporting self-assessment.

- I have a secure understanding of how learners learn and have made realistic judgements about my impact on the progress of individual learners.

3

DEMONSTRATE GOOD SUBJECT AND CURRICULUM KNOWLEDGE

3 A teacher must: demonstrate good subject and curriculum knowledge

A   have a secure knowledge of the relevant subject(s) and curriculum areas, foster and maintain pupils' interest in the subject and address misunderstandings

B   demonstrate a critical understanding of developments in the subject and curriculum areas, and promote the value of scholarship

C   demonstrate an understanding of and take responsibility for promoting high standards of literacy, articulacy and the correct use of standard English, whatever the teacher's specialist subject

D   if teaching early reading, demonstrate a clear understanding of systematic synthetic phonics

E   if teaching early mathematics, demonstrate a clear understanding of appropriate teaching strategies.

(DfE, 2012a, pp7-8)

COMMENTARY

If you ask pupils what makes a good teacher it is quite likely they will reply, 'they love their subject'. Indeed, for many teachers, what draws them into the profession is a passion for the subject and a deep interest in children and young people. Standard 3 highlights the fundamental importance of good teaching underpinned by secure knowledge of the subject and the wider curriculum.

As in other aspects of the Teachers' Standards, there are self-evident differences when relating this Standard to a particular age group. The teacher of five-year-olds needs to demonstrate one kind of command of a range of subjects and topics, combined with a deep understanding of child development. The secondary teacher must demonstrate a command of their subject which will extend the intellects of pupils from 11-18.

In amplifying the scope of the Standard 3 heading, there are five stated areas for teachers to focus upon.

A There are three clauses to be noted here. The first pinpoints a secure knowledge of subject and curriculum area, a reminder that keeping up-to-date with the latest developments in a subject is an important tool of the teacher's professionalism. Second, the skilled teacher, building on their knowledge of individual pupils' talents and aptitudes, will introduce ideas and activities that foster new and renewed lines of enquiry. Thirdly, the astute teacher is quick to spot where misunderstandings have occurred, and takes appropriate action to intervene and re-explain a challenging concept or skill.

B Effective teachers not only keep abreast of the latest developments in their subject, but they are adept at analysing and selecting wisely for classroom use those new techniques, research findings and resources which will have the greatest impact on those they teach. In turn, pupils are quick to recognise those teachers who really know their subject and are able to value and promote 'scholarship'. It is worth commenting that while on the surface we might at first associate the word 'scholarship' with an A-level seminar on *Othello*, the accomplished Year 4 teacher exploring 200 million-year-old fossils can soon bring alive the Jurassic coastline of west Dorset in a way that inspires pupils.

C All teaching and learning is rooted in effective communication. How teachers model the use of language, in all its richness, has a telling impact on young minds. Whatever teachers' academic backgrounds, they have a pivotal responsibility to model and promote high standards in the usage of English. At one level, this requires teachers to think about the specialist keywords of their subject. At another, it means correcting pupils' misuse of grammar in written assignments. And, sensitively carried through with respect for accent and dialect, it means the teacher intervening to ensure that pupils speak clearly and correctly.

There are important training implications for the whole profession within this aspect of Standard 3.

D   The wording here is important: 'if teaching early reading'. At first glance, this appears to be aimed at teachers of younger children. On reflection, it is a stark fact that teachers in the early years of secondary school may also be encountering pupils with faltering reading skills. While some pupils arrive in primary school able to read and demonstrate enjoyment in handling books, many do not. Those in the profession with responsibilities for early reading must have at their command a secure understanding of the key features and practice of systematic synthetic phonics. They must, for example, have a secure understanding of the importance for beginner readers of grapheme-phoneme correspondence, blending phonemes and segmenting words.

E   An echo of the previous point: 'if teaching early mathematics'. While the emphasis in relation to reading is on a particular approach, here the expectation is that teachers will have a secure grasp of a range of suitable teaching techniques when working on mathematics. For example, practical, hands-on experiences of using, comparing and calculating with numbers and quantities and the development of mental methods are of crucial importance in establishing the best mathematical start in primary up to Year 6. Coupled with this, pupils need plenty of opportunities for developing mathematical language so that they learn to express their thinking using the correct vocabulary.

REFLECTIONS

1.   What regular reading and internet researching do you do to ensure that you are up-to-date with the latest developments in the subject and curriculum areas you teach?

2.   Which particular techniques and ideas have you harnessed to foster pupils' interest in a subject?

3.   Think of an example where you have intervened successfully with a pupil to address a misunderstanding they had about a skill or concept. How did you help the pupil understand and then move on with confidence to tackle a fresh challenge?

(Continued)

(Continued)

4. What examples have you seen in other teachers' classrooms of materials and ideas which promote real scholarship?

5. What are your own professional strengths when modelling best usage in English, orally and in writing? Do you have any particular training needs?

6. How do you promote articulacy in your own classroom? What expectations do you have when pupils are speaking?

7. For those involved in early reading and mathematics in primary schools: what best practice have you observed and learned from?

8. For those teaching early reading and early mathematics in secondary schools: what best practice have you seen in the special needs department which you might bring to your own classroom?

EVIDENCE

Demonstrate evidence to your tutor/mentor of:

- recent and relevant background reading related to your classroom practice;
- classroom displays and/or internet material which reflect topical developments or contemporary issues and debate in your subject;
- examples of materials you have created to foster pupils' interests;
- lesson plans which explicitly reference the 'value of scholarship';
- examples of your marking which focus on pupils' literacy usage;
- where appropriate, classroom practice which demonstrates your ability to teach systematic synthetic phonics and early mathematics with skill and precision.

EXAMPLE OF GOOD PRACTICE

Interactive phonics teaching

Sarah worked with a Reception class which included some children with English as an additional language. She was working with them on developing their phonological awareness in preparation for moving on to look at graphemes and phonemes. This meant doing a lot of work on sounds and helping children to discriminate between sounds.

Sarah created a 'sound box' into which she could place items which could be used to make a variety of sounds, including a box of sweets, a bag of crisps, a jar of marbles, a triangle, maracas and a tambourine. She made the sounds for the children and then let them take turns to make the sounds as they passed them around. Then she put the items in the box so that they could not see them and made the sounds and asked the children to identify the items making them.

Sarah introduced a range of interactive activities involving sounds, including a 'sounds walk' around the school which she recorded and then played back, asking children to say where they heard different sounds. She also played 'sounds I-spy', in which she and the children 'spied' things beginning with different phonemes rather than letters. When getting children to line up, do jobs, etc., she often used the initial phonemes of names, for example: 'Everyone whose name begins with /sss/ come and sit down, please.'

When using animal noises as part of singing *Old MacDonald Had a Farm*, Sarah asked children to make the sound that they associated with different animals and found that for dogs, in particular, there was a range and that many of the EAL children used sounds other than the traditional 'wuff'. Sarah also invited parents and carers to come into the classroom to help with singing and found that this was well-received by some whose English was developing, especially when they were able to contribute sound effects to songs.

STANDARD 3: DEMONSTRATE GOOD SUBJECT AND CURRICULUM KNOWLEDGE

Have I met Standard 3?

- I have a secure subject-related pedagogical knowledge and understanding of the relevant subject.

- I can answer learners' questions confidently and fully.

- I can foster and maintain pupils' interest.

- I know and can respond to learners' common misconceptions.

- I have a sufficiently secure knowledge and understanding of relevant initiatives – at local and national levels.

- I can promote the value of pupils' further learning.

- I can locate relevant resources to help me improve my teaching and wider professional activities.

- I know the ways that learners can be supported in developing literacy across the curriculum.

INTERLUDE: VISITING AN EARLY YEARS' SETTING

Read through questions 1-14, which aim to help you reflect on and analyse best practice.

(a) When you visit a colleague's Nursery or Reception classroom, use the following questions as a checklist against which you make observations.

(b) At the end of a given week, use the questions to help you reflect on your own best practice and where you might wish to fine-tune your own classroom.

(c) Add your own questions to the checklist as you develop your own skills in lesson observation.

The learning environment

1. Do the outdoor and indoor spaces engage children's interest across all the areas of learning expected in the early years?

2. Does the learning environment provide challenge and extend children's skills and understanding?

3. Are the furniture and learning resources of high quality and in excellent condition?

4. Is children's work displayed to show it is valued, of high quality and diverse?

Relationships

5. Are children's learning and social needs fully supported by adults?

6. Are there effective and warm relationships between parents and their child's key person?

7. Do children have warm and positive relationships with each other? Do they help each other?

Quality of learning

8. Are observations recorded, regularly assessed and used to inform short-term plans?

9. Do staff plan for individual children's next steps of learning, for example in phonics and in number work?

10. Are planned activities interesting, inspiring and appropriate to age and stage of development?

11. Are children provided with achievable challenges and are new and exciting activities on offer?

12. Is the daily routine flexible to allow for spontaneous events?

13. Is knowledge of children's preferences and needs used to maximise children's progress?

14. Are individual needs met, e.g. for those with special educational needs or who are especially talented?

4

PLAN AND TEACH WELL-STRUCTURED LESSONS

4   A teacher must: plan and teach well-structured lessons

A   impart knowledge and develop understanding through effective use of lesson time

B   promote a love of learning and children's intellectual curiosity

C   set homework and plan other out-of-class activities to consolidate and extend the knowledge and understanding pupils have acquired

D   reflect systematically on the effectiveness of lessons and approaches to teaching

E   contribute to the design and provision of an engaging curriculum within the relevant subject area(s).

(DfE, 2012a, p8)

COMMENTARY

The first three Standards lay out fair and challenging professional foundations: effective teachers possess a love of a subject or subjects they know well combined with an enthusiasm for working with young people; they have consistently high

(Continued)

(Continued)

expectations of those they teach; and they expect their pupils to make good progress and outcomes. Standard 4 focuses on the craft of the classroom: what is it that is involved in planning and teaching well-structured lessons, something that is as important to the teacher in their first year of practice as it is to the senior member of staff in their twentieth year? What is the cocktail of the good lesson?

In amplifying the scope of the Standard 4 heading, there are five stated areas for teachers to focus upon.

A The teacher, as adult and trained professional, has a body of knowledge to impart. Pupils know and expect this to be the case. Furthermore, pupils look to their teacher to share that knowledge with enthusiasm, passion and a keen eye for what will motivate them. At the heart of learning something new is developing an understanding, to the point where the pupil can teach something they have learned well to someone else. To teach is to learn. Skilled teachers orchestrate lesson time adroitly. They combine their own explanations and interventions with setting aside sufficient time for pupils to explore new ideas and embed understanding. Information technology may play a critical and increasing role here.

B All classrooms need to be rooted in the fun and fundamentals of learning. Teachers must give their pupils the opportunity to enjoy what they are doing as well as appreciating that mastery of a new topic or skill lies in purposeful practice, occasional failure and 'crying intellectually' before eventual success. The old motto resonates in most classrooms: 'If at first you don't succeed, try, try again.' Good teachers organise their classrooms and lessons in ways which stimulate curious minds and promote a love of learning for its own sake as well as how that learning can be applied beyond school. This links to the use of the word 'scholarship' in Standard 3.

C Pupils will tell you that most teachers, from time to time, set homework at the last minute in a lesson because the homework timetable says they must. Good practice lies in lesson planning which integrates classwork and homework wisely so that pupils see the purpose of devoting evening and weekend time to consolidating and extending what they have learned in class. The examination years in secondary school certainly require pupils to be well organised in managing independent study time, so good habits established in primary school are valued by pupils and parents alike.

This sets further expectations around out-of-class activities, highlighting the importance of school visits and other extra-curricular experiences to enrich the curriculum.

D In both Standards 2 and 3, teachers are expected to reflect self-critically on practice. It is the hallmark of any good professional: seeking to do something better tomorrow than they did it today. The reflective practitioner is nowhere more important than in this arena of daily practice in the classroom. What did I do today with that high ability maths group which really worked well? Why did I run out of time with that debate activity? What was it about that home-work assignment that led to every pupil handing it back by the deadline set? How can I encourage more pupils to present their written work with greater attention to legibility?

E   Whether a trainee teacher or one with many years' experience, you gradu-ally develop a rich bank of tried and tested teaching materials. Many teachers use laptops for lesson planning, sharing what has gone well and less well with colleagues on a daily or weekly basis. Aside from the impor-tance of sharing best practice, this interchange of ideas and materials serves to keep under active revision the curriculum on offer. One of the most excit-ing aspects of teaching is scrutinising subject content and amending it in the light of experience. Indeed, some teachers get into writing textbooks that way! Teachers new to the profession have much to contribute to ensuring that the curriculum proves engaging and relevant to pupils.

REFLECTIONS

1.   What particular personal and professional strengths do you bring to your classroom? Do you have a passion for teaching a particular age range or subject matter?

2.   What practice have you seen where a teacher has made skilful use of time, for example enabling pupils to build deep learning following on from a teacher's expert introduction?

3.   The phrase 'crying intellectually' has been used above to stimulate the reader's thinking. Which teaching techniques do you use to ensure that pupils grapple and persevere with challenging tasks?

4.   What examples have you seen in colleagues' classrooms of exciting and innovative approaches to homework which inspire pupils?

5.   What particular activities (e.g. visitors into class, visits out, forging business and community partners) would you enjoy organising to enhance pupils' learning?

(Continued)

(*Continued*)

6. Think about a couple of lessons you have taught which have exceeded your expectations in terms of superb response from pupils. And think of two lessons where you had to work much harder than the pupils and their responses were limited. Which teaching approaches did you use which proved (a) particularly successful and (b) less profitable? What lessons did you learn as a reflective practitioner?

7. What is your preferred format for creating and recording lesson plans? What opportunities do you have to share your plans with colleagues and to look at theirs in order to share best practice?

8. Where do you feel you are making/will be able to make the most significant contribution to your school's curriculum development planning?

EVIDENCE

Demonstrate evidence to your tutor/mentor of:

- lesson plans which indicate skilful orchestration of time;
- teaching which demonstrates well-judged interventions which serve to develop pupils' understanding;
- teaching which promotes pupils' love of learning;
- materials and tasks which stimulate intellectual curiosity;
- homework activities which consolidate new learning in a motivating and purposeful way for pupils;
- examples of lesson plans you have amended in the light of teaching experience;
- your contributions to curriculum design and development.

STANDARD 4: PLAN AND TEACH WELL STRUCTURED LESSONS

Have I met Standard 4?

- I have selected and adapted my teaching style and strategy to suit the stage of the lesson, and the needs of individuals in my class.

- I have drawn on a range of relevant resources when planning, and considered the age and ability range of the learners in my class.

- I have used accurate assessments of learners' progress to inform planning.

- I have built on learners' prior experience and planned for a personalised learning approach.

- I have supported and encouraged children to manage aspects of their own learning thus challenging them so that they enjoy learning for themselves.

- I have managed the timing and pace of lessons and intervened effectively to support learning.

- I have managed unexpected 'changes of direction' or 'shifts in emphasis' within the lesson and over time.

- Homework – I have planned homework to take account of learners' attainment, needs and interests.

- I have designed, planned and assessed homework to consolidate and extend learning and offered feedback.

- I have used self-reviewing procedures to identify specific ways of improving my practice.

5

ADAPT TEACHING TO RESPOND TO THE STRENGTHS AND NEEDS OF ALL PUPILS

5   A teacher must: adapt teaching to respond to the strengths and needs of all pupils

A   know when and how to differentiate appropriately, using approaches which enable pupils to be taught effectively

B   have a secure understanding of how a range of factors can inhibit pupils' ability to learn and how best to overcome these

C   demonstrate an awareness of the physical, social and intellectual development of children and know how to adapt teaching to support pupils' education at different stages of development

D   have a clear understanding of the needs of all pupils, including those with special educational needs; those of high ability; those with English as an additional language; those with disabilities; and be able to use and evaluate distinctive teaching approaches to engage and support them.

(DfE, 2012a, p8)

COMMENTARY

One of the striking features of any class of pupils is the sheer diversity and range of interests, aptitudes, aspirations and attitudes towards learning. This is at times memorable, frustrating, enriching and confusing. Standard 5 sets out the clear expectation that teaching needs to be adapted to respond to the strengths and weaknesses of all pupils. This is demanding, whether for the trainee teacher or the experienced practitioner.

The key word 'differentiate' is used by classroom observers (whether colleagues, tutors or inspectors) offering feedback on lessons. In fact, the word's regular appearance in the context of feedback highlights just how difficult it can be for even the most skilled teacher to ensure that the needs of *all* pupils are met consistently.

In amplifying the scope of the Standard 5 heading, there are four stated areas for the teacher to focus upon.

A   Whether teaching a so-called mixed-ability or setted or banded class, a range of abilities will always exist. Whole-class teaching nearly always has its place, and within that mode of instruction, skilful and open questioning can serve to differentiate effectively. Well judged interventions from the teacher are a hall-mark of very good teaching, in any context, from the practical to the more intellectual. The constant challenge for the teacher is knowing when and how to differentiate: at what point in a session to pause to allow independent working; which pupils should work together as a group; which individuals would benefit from focused attention from a learning support assistant; which pupils might gain from following up a question through use of the internet or a self-study program on the laptop; which pair might go off to the library; how best (and when) to use a mini-plenary, led by the teacher or a group of pupils; can homework be usefully differentiated?

B   Knowing pupils' individual learning needs is both explicit and implicit within a number of the Standards. The skilled professional will have a secure knowl-edge of how different factors can inhibit learning, and what techniques and interventions can be deployed in the best interests of the pupils. Of course, the factors may change in the course of a term or year, and the aware teacher is alert to that change. For some pupils, challenging home circum-stances may mean that the school sets aside good facilities for those pupils to do homework. Additional one-to-one reading groups may be needed by other pupils, or catch-up classes in maths. Tracking and evaluating the impact of interventions is essential.

C   Self-evidently, pupils develop at different rates and in different ways, physically, socially and intellectually. Skilled early years' practitioners can recognise when young children move from a simple understanding of the concrete to appreciating abstract ideas. Secondary teachers will make perceptive judgements about when to introduce certain challenging and perhaps 'adult' concepts. While working within the programmes outlined in the National Curriculum, school-based curriculum or examination syllabuses, confident teachers make selections about content on a regular basis, tailoring subject matter and new skills to the needs of their pupils.

D This point builds carefully on the previous three, with a particular focus on four groups of pupils, appreciating always that groups are made up of individuals. There is emphasis too on teachers harnessing distinctive approaches in classrooms, and evaluating their impact, making adjustments as required.

Group 1: teachers in mainstream settings encounter some pupils who find learning in their particular subject difficult. This may be linked to delayed cognitive development, to a pupil's hand-eye coordination, to difficulties with speech or handwriting, or to temporary medical problems. The onus is on the teacher (and the school) to have diagnosed the specific learning needs and to have put in place strategies to address them.

Further, it is the responsibility of all teachers to act on an individual pupil's school action plan or statement of special educational needs which might specify different writing equipment, a bespoke space in the classroom with additional lighting, a short note to parents in a pupil's diary at the end of each lesson or extra time for practical assignments.

Group 2: the education system has often been unhelpful to teachers in the way it has requested schools to identify so-called 'gifted and talented' pupils and to place them on a special register. Schools sometimes miss out on identifying pupils' particular talents. Pupils' individual needs must be catered for whether by the Year 5 teacher who finds two very able mathematicians in her class; or the Year 10 teacher who has two outstanding gymnasts in his GCSE PE class; or the Year 12 teacher who has in her A level English group a potential Oxbridge scholar.

Group 3: there are significant numbers of pupils in UK schools whose first language is not English (EAL pupils) and whose working knowledge of English varies considerably. Widespread evidence indicates that this fact is rarely an obstacle to good progress and outcomes if teachers are suitably trained in EAL teaching techniques. Recognition of the pupils' heritage language(s) is vital and, for example, dual-language dictionaries may be provided in class. Equally critical is the teacher's determination to provide scaffolding and support to accelerate pupils' oral and written command of English: the language of school, examinations, university and the workplace ahead.

(Continued)

(Continued)

Group 4: it is important to remember here that disabilities in pupils can be temporary or more permanent, each requiring different, sensitively thought-through approaches. In most schools there are specialists who are able to offer appropriate advice to colleagues and trainee teachers are strongly advised to avail themselves of this expertise. For teachers in special schools, clearly a complex array of special needs presents itself, requiring tailored interventions rooted in high-quality training, and working in a multi-professional classroom.

REFLECTIONS

1. From your own school days, which subject do you remember being particularly good at, or having difficulties with? What interventions and support do you recall as being most effective for you?

2. When first meeting a class, what techniques do you use to gauge pupils' different aptitudes and interests? How do you use the school's pupil performance data to help you?

3. When you are giving an introduction to a topic or detailed explanation to a whole class, how do you check they have understood what you have been saying? Think about your natural style of questioning - is it suitably open?

4. What practice have you observed from other colleagues which enables skilful differentiation within whole-class teaching sessions?

5. What practice have you seen which leads to very good differentiation through individual, paired or small group work? Which teaching and learning techniques have you introduced in your own classroom that have been particularly effective?

6. Reflect on an occasion when you have been successful in adapting your teaching as a response to your keen awareness of a group of pupils' social or intellectual development. What did you do that had a strong impact?

7. For those pupils with a statement of educational needs, which interventions have you seen in colleagues' classrooms that you have judged to be having a significant impact on pupils' progress and outcomes?

8. For high attaining pupils, what materials and interventions have you seen in other classrooms which have impressed you, and which you would like to emulate?

9. What are your own specific training needs to support your teaching of pupils whose first language is not English?

10. Turning back to Standard 1 (see p9), how do you ensure, within your classroom teaching, that you set consistently high expectations for pupils with special educational needs?

EVIDENCE

Demonstrate evidence to your tutor/mentor of:

- displays which profile the work of pupils of high ability;
- displays which profile the work of pupils with special educational needs or disabilities;
- lesson plans which specify how you are differentiating tasks for high-ability pupils;
- classroom and homework materials which cater for the needs of those pupils with English as an additional language;
- your classroom actions in response to a pupil's statement of special educational needs, including, where appropriate, effective deployment of a learning support assistant;
- questioning techniques which demonstrate skilful differentiation.

STANDARD 5: ADAPT TEACHING TO RESPOND TO THE STRENGTH AND NEEDS OF ALL PUPILS

Have I met Standard 5?

- I have considered the range of learners' needs through an inclusive approach.

- I have identified learners' needs and differentiated tasks, activities and resources effectively to support individuals and groups of learners including those with special educational needs, those with disabilities, those for whom English is an additional language and those from diverse social, cultural, ethnic, religious and linguistic backgrounds.

- I have understood and am able to use the progress made by individual learners in a lesson or sequence of lessons and identify personalised targets for future lessons.

- I have been able to use the impact of the design and content of the curriculum in meeting learners' needs, and the extent to which teaching strategies and resources can be modified to provide for personalised learning.

- I have been able to use the principles and techniques of formative assessment in order to meet the needs of all learners.

- I have found out about, and considered the key factors that contribute to the development, progress and well-being of learners (including drawing on evidence from a range of stakeholders).

- I have been aware of the whole-school ethos and policies, procedures and approaches relating to the range of factors that can affect learning and well-being.

- I have been aware of the extent to which different backgrounds and influences may impact learning both positively and negatively.

- I have known who to refer to for support and advice on EAL including bilingual learners, SEN, disability and diversity, and how to utilise the advice and support.

- I have understood the connection between a child's behaviour and changes or difficulties in their personal circumstances.

INTERLUDE: VISITING A YEAR 2 CLASSROOM

Read through questions 1-15, which aim to help you reflect on and analyse best practice.

(a) When you visit a colleague's Year 2 classroom, use the following questions as a checklist against which you make observations.

(b) At the end of a given week, use the questions to help you reflect on your own best practice, and where you might wish to fine-tune your own classroom.

(c) Add your own questions to the checklist as you develop your own skills in lesson observation.

The learning environment

1. Do the outdoor and indoor spaces engage children's interest across all the areas of learning expected in Year 2?

2. Does the learning environment include interactive displays which can be used for reference by the children?

3. Are the furniture and learning resources arranged appropriately for different activities?

4. Is children's work displayed to show it is valued, of high quality and diverse?

Relationships

5. Are children's learning and social needs fully supported by adults?

6. Are there effective and warm relationships with parents and carers?

7. Do children have warm and positive relationships with each other? Do they help each other?

Quality of learning

8. Are observations recorded, regularly assessed and used to inform short-term plans?

9. Do staff plan for individual children's next steps of learning, for example in phonics and in number work?

10. Are planned activities interesting, inspiring and appropriate to age and stage of development?

11. Do the teacher and any teaching assistants model activities for children so that they know what is expected of them?

12. Are children provided with achievable challenges and new and exciting activities on offer?

13. Is there a strong emphasis on reading for pleasure?

14. Is knowledge of children's interests and needs used to maximise children's progress?

15. Are individual needs met, e.g. for those with special educational needs or who are especially talented?

6

MAKE ACCURATE AND PRODUCTIVE USE OF ASSESSMENT

6   A teacher must: make accurate and productive use of assessment

A   know and understand how to assess the relevant subject and curriculum areas, including statutory assessment requirements

B   make use of formative and summative assessment to secure pupils' progress

C   use relevant data to monitor progress, set targets and plan subsequent lessons

D   give pupils regular feedback, both orally and through accurate marking, and encourage pupils to respond to the feedback.

(DfE, 2012a, p8)

———— COMMENTARY ————

Standard 1 sets down expectations that teachers are accountable for pupils' progress and outcomes. Pivotal to this is a teacher's accurate and productive use of assessment. In common with school systems globally, the explosion of available data and ways of analysing performance within UK schools has given rise to a

(Continued)

(Continued)

whole industry of target setting, benchmarking and national and international league tables. This plethora of information can sometimes threaten to overwhelm the teacher. It is important, therefore, to have a secure grasp of meaningful and relevant data which impacts on your own teaching at classroom level.

In amplifying the scope of the Standard 6 heading, there are four stated areas for teachers to focus upon.

A   Standard 3 outlines the importance of the teacher's good subject and curriculum knowledge. Building on that knowledge in this Standard comes the expectation that a teacher has a secure grasp of how pupils are to be assessed in a given curriculum area: whether as a Reception practitioner involved with the early learning goals, a Year 8 geography teacher ensuring coverage of environmental change and sustainable development or a Year 11 teacher of design and technology ensuring sufficient time is allocated to students' coursework.

This point further highlights the vital importance of teachers knowing well the particular statutory assessment requirements relevant to the age range they are teaching, from phonics tests at age 6 to A level papers at age 18.

B   The words 'formative' and 'summative' are part of every teacher's vocabulary – and it is important to have a clear understanding of the difference between the two. In essence:

- 'formative' is about informing and shaping the pupil's ongoing work and the teacher's knowledge of those developments. Formative assessment takes place all the time in class as teachers circulate and correct pupils' work, orally and in writing, and the more experienced the teacher often the more seamless it appears;

- 'summative' comes at the end of a unit, or term, or year, offering a judgement – and usually a grade or mark – on work completed. Summative assessment requires teachers to know their subjects well and be in a position to apply test or examination criteria to pupils' completed assignments without fear or favour.

C   When used well by teachers, data can have a powerful impact on pupils' progress and overall school improvement. The key for schools and teachers is applying a 'less is more' approach, so that everyone involved has a clear understanding of which data is relevant and which is superfluous. The mark book (whether on paper or online) is every teacher's stock-in-trade, importantly recording pupils' prior attainment data, for example reading ages, cognitive ability test scores, or National Curriculum expectations attained. The same mark book will include individual targets for pupils which are both challenging and plausible, and which have been agreed as part of a whole-school policy on rigorous target-setting.

This evolving data is used not only to record progress and outcomes but also, importantly, to inform future lesson planning, including differentiating tasks and assignments to best match pupils' strengths and needs.

D   Feedback is the fuel that propels every pupil's learning. Ask a class of Year 6 or Year 11 pupils what they value about their teacher and prompt, high-quality marking will be close to top of the list. 'Marking' in music, physical education, design and technology, history or English comes in different forms, but at the heart of effective classrooms is the teacher's determination to comment on strengths and identify next steps in the best interests of the pupil. Oral feedback can be just as valuable as written. A key adjective here is 'regular' – marking needs to be prompt, regular and focused, and is usually shaped by whole-school or departmental guidance.

Finally, teachers spend a lot of time marking and making comments in exercise books and folders. Ask yourself the question: do I give enough time to the pupils to read what I have written? The answer is too often 'no'. Pupils need to have time set aside to respond to the teacher's feedback if they are to progress.

REFLECTIONS

1.   What national and international benchmarking of pupils and schools systems do you know about, for example PISA and TIMMS? How does your school use this benchmarking?

2.   How are pupils in your school performing in the core subjects of English and mathematics relative to local and national statistics?

3.   Reflect on how performance data is used in your school. Do you have a secure grasp of the data which is relevant to your classroom? Do you have any training needs, for example with understanding Raiseonline (the Ofsted/DfE interactive system, Reporting and Analysis for Improvement through School Self-Evaluation)?

4.   What background reading have you done to ensure you have a good command of statutory assessments relevant to the pupils you are teaching? What in-service training have you had to help you with moderation of pupils' work and summative assessment?

(Continued)

(Continued)

5. Observing in other classrooms, what practice have you seen in 'formative' assessment which has impressed you? How does the skilled teacher embed the process of formative assessment into classroom practice?

6. Which habits are you establishing in accurate record-keeping of pupils' performance data? Is your recording set out in such a way that, if you were absent for a week, a colleague could understand its contents? Could your line manager use it to gain a quick overview of pupils' progress in your class?

7. What kind of target-setting have you done which pupils find useful and motivating? What good practice have you seen in colleagues' classrooms?

8. What examples of 'next-best-step' marking in English and mathematics have you been shown or seen through observations?

9. Reflect on your emerging management of marking records. What habits of good time management are you establishing?

EVIDENCE

Demonstrate evidence to your tutor/mentor of:

- your knowledge of your school's overall performance data;
- your knowledge of data relevant to the pupils you are teaching;
- a mark book (or similar) which has detailed and accurate records of pupils' progress and performance;
- lesson plans which have been adapted and differentiated in the light of assessments you have made of pupils' work;
- good quality 'next-best-step' marking;
- in your classroom practice, good examples of formative assessment, oral and in writing.

STANDARD 6: MAKE ACCURATE AND PRODUCTIVE USE OF ASSESSMENT

Have I met Standard 6?

- I have engaged in discussion with experienced colleagues about assessment requirements and arrangements.

- I am aware of how to moderate and interpret assessments and apply this in practice.

- I am able to use my awareness and understanding of assessment requirements and arrangements in my planning and teaching.

- I have become familiar with ways of preparing learners for assessment activities and this is apparent in my practice.

- I am familiar with the national expectations for pupils in the subject, and how learners make progress, based on an understanding of available data sets.

- I know and understand how to apply a range of assessment strategies in different contexts and for different purposes.

- I know and understand how and why formative assessment can improve learning outcomes and attainment.

- I am familiar with knowing and understanding the value of oral and written feedback and how to apply this to practice, engaging learners with feedback.

- I know and understand the ways that immediate feedback can reinforce learning, challenge understanding, construct ways forward and help learners to improve. *It is applied in my practice.*

- I know and understand the impact of my feedback – for example, on learner engagement, enthusiasm and confidence.

- I know and understand the need for learners to understand the purposes of tasks and activities, and how this understanding can support self- and peer assessment.

- I know and understand the benefits of involving learners in the assessment of their own learning.

- I know and understand how assessment relates to intended learning outcomes and use this to generate learners' targets.

- I know how to set realistic targets for achievement based on the pupil-level data available to me.

- I have been able to demonstrate how statistical information can be used to differentiate my teaching and to personalise learning.

- I know how to assess learners and set them targets against their achievement of intended learning outcomes (and national benchmarks).

- I have involved learners in setting objectives for the development of their own learning.

- I have provided immediate feedback in order to reinforce learning, challenge understanding, construct ways forward and help all groups of learners to improve.

- I have provided oral and written feedback that is accurate and constructive, securing learner engagement and confidence.

- I have used a range of assessment strategies, and demonstrated an understanding of the impact of formative assessment.

INTERLUDE: VISITING A YEAR 6 CLASSROOM

Read through questions 1–12, which aim to help you reflect on and analyse best practice.

(a) When you visit a colleague's upper primary classroom, use the following questions as a checklist against which you make observations.

(b) At the end of a given week, use the questions to help you reflect on your own best practice, and where you might wish to fine-tune your own classroom.

(c) Add your own questions to the checklist as you develop your skills and experiences.

Questions to ask

1. What are your first impressions of the learning environment?

   - Is it light, airy and the right temperature for learning?

   - Does the classroom, and the areas around it, reflect the range of Y6/upper primary work? What is special or striking about this work?

   - Is the classroom arranged so that all children can be involved in discussions and also use their workspace to write, design and implement?

   - How do the children react to your presence as a visitor? To what extent are they happy to talk and explain?

   - Is it clear that the Y6 class is not merely involved in a SATs revision exercise – or, if this is the case, how is this being managed to maximise learning?

2. In what ways does the style of teaching and learning reflect that this is a Year 6 class and therefore distinctive in terms of the completion of the primary stage of learning?

3. How is the furniture configured? Are children sitting on the carpet for too long? Where does the teacher position her/himself?

4. To what extent do the children take control of their learning and how able are they to explore a range of learning areas? Are the children aware of what will come next in terms of their move to the secondary stage?

5. In the time you are in the room, count the minutes (a) the teacher talks and (b) children converse with a proper focus. Is the teacher working harder than the students? Are the children responding easily and readily to the task/stimuli provided?

6. How are support staff being deployed to have a significant impact on learning?

7. What evidence can you see of Year 6's independent learning skills? If the teacher left the room, would the children continue to work on the current task?

8. Is the level of work appropriate for the more able learners and is it sufficiently demanding? Has the work been effectively scaffolded while retaining an intrinsic interest/challenge for those who have learning or personal management difficulties?

9. Is homework or other independent study/research important to the lesson being observed? Has there been some form of lead-in and are there possibilities for extension?

10. How creatively are book/technology resources harnessed to stimulate students' interest and extend their skills and knowledge?

11. Can you tell from looking at books/folders whether the children fully understand what is expected from this lesson/topic? Is there a difference in the way that girls and boys approach this lesson?

12. Are targets for individuals and groups in place? Do the children clearly understand what is expected of them? Is the marking formative and helpful to the child so that s/he can progress?

7

MANAGE BEHAVIOUR EFFECTIVELY TO ENSURE A GOOD AND SAFE LEARNING ENVIRONMENT

7   A teacher must: manage behaviour effectively to ensure a good and safe learning environment

A   have clear rules and routines for behaviour in classrooms and take responsibility for promoting good and courteous behaviour both in classrooms and around the school in accordance with the school's behaviour policy

B   have high expectations of behaviour and establish a framework for discipline with a range of strategies, using praise, sanctions and rewards consistently and fairly

C   manage classes effectively, using approaches which are appropriate to pupils' needs in order to involve and motivate them

D   maintain good relationships with pupils, exercise appropriate authority and act decisively when necessary.

(DfE, 2012a, p8)

————— COMMENTARY —————

All around the world parents send their children to school each day. Ask any parent what they expect of a school and a likely reply will be that they expect their child to be safe, happy and well looked after. Learning will follow.

(Continued)

(Continued)

It is important for teachers to remember that they are *in loco parentis* at all times and thus have a core responsibility for ensuring a good and safe learning environment. For some pupils, schools provide a stability and welcoming environment that they may not always experience at home.

When pupils feel secure in their school environment, their self-esteem and motivation are lifted and they are more likely to be ready for positive learning and engagement with their teachers. This is as true of a young child in Year 1 as it is of a sixth-former in his last year of college.

In amplifying the scope of the Standard 7 heading, there are four stated areas for teachers to focus upon.

A   There are a number of aspects here which are built on in the subsequent points. One clear expectation comes in the phrase 'in accordance with the school's behaviour policy', a reminder that teachers need to act consistently within an overall school framework if behaviour is to be well managed. Remember: pupils thrive on a consistency of approach and are quick to exploit inconsistencies. Rules and routines are often set down at a whole-school level and it is important that they are followed through by individual teachers. In good schools, pupils and staff treat each other with dignity, courteously, whether in classrooms, corridors or playgrounds. Every teacher has his or her part to play.

B   In the same way that Standard 1 talks of high expectations which motivate pupils, teachers need to demonstrate at all times that they have high expectations of pupils' behaviours and attitudes to learning. Pupils very often have a strong sense of right and wrong – and are quick to express their feelings on the subject – so it is vital that sanctions and rewards are applied consistently and fairly. Trainee teachers might well be given a mentor on the staff to help them with this. There is another word here which requires thoughtful interpretation: 'praise'. It is important that when praise is given, it is earned, and not given for something trivial or which other pupils perceive as undeserved. This is not an easy balance to get right every day, but it is critical to do so to ensure a positive discipline framework.

C   Within a consistent and well applied discipline framework, teachers manage classes in many different ways, and rightly so as this aspect of teaching is closely linked to a teacher's individual personality. What might work for one teacher may not for another, although it is always instructive to observe how skilful staff manage challenging pupils. Whatever strategies are employed, the focus is on involving and motivating pupils to learn and gain maximum benefit from the lessons.

Among many features that might be listed, the following are worth noting when observing others and reflecting on one's own practice: the teacher's body language and voice projection; the teacher's position and movement around the classroom; room temperature and light; the teacher's knowledge of every pupil's name; rules around talking and listening; managing transitions; accessibility to pupils of resources; the appearance of the teacher's own desk and the storage of pupils' books; furniture configuration; designated seating plans. Most schools have a checklist of helpful, school-specific tips to support new teachers.

D Good teaching is built upon teachers establishing a professional and personal rapport with those they teach. This varies depending on the age of the pupils but lies at the core of a successful classroom. There is no substitute for humour, warmth and well-judged challenge and support, delivered in a tone of voice that at once shows the pupils that the teacher cares and is being fair in their dealings. Even the youngest pupils are quick to recognise the teacher who talks down to them, while teenagers can be rightly riled by indiscriminate sarcasm from teachers.

Further, this point is worded carefully in expecting teachers to 'exercise appropriate authority' and 'act decisively'. Individual schools will give guidance on this, highlighting the need to act professionally and promptly where the occasion arises.

REFLECTIONS

1. What is your understanding of the phrase *in loco parentis* as it applies in your school context?

2. What evidence have you seen of pupils reacting well to a good, welcoming environment and reacting negatively to a poor environment?

3. Reading through your school's behaviour policy, what seem to be its strengths and perhaps weaknesses? Which aspects of the policy seem to be most effective with pupils? Are pupils involved in keeping the policy under review?

4. What have you learned from observing colleagues about how (a) sanctions and (b) praise are used to positive effect?

(Continued)

(Continued)

5. Reflect on the list of features in point C above – what techniques are you developing to ensure good classroom management?

6. Think of examples in your school setting (and on school visits) where you have been or might be called upon to 'act decisively' and 'exercise appropriate authority'.

7. The following is taken from the Ofsted school inspection handbook. It describes what the features are of a school where behaviour and attitudes to learning are outstanding. What do you think of these descriptors as applied to your own school and classroom? Would you amend or add anything to these descriptors, given Ofsted revises and updates them on a regular basis?

OUTSTANDING (1)

- Pupils behave with consistently high levels of respect for others. They play a highly positive role in creating a school environment in which commonalities are identified and celebrated, difference is valued and nurtured, and bullying, harassment and violence are never tolerated.

- Pupils consistently have highly positive attitudes and commitment to their education. They are highly motivated and persistent in the face of difficulties. Pupils make a highly positive, tangible contribution to the life of the school and/or the wider community. Pupils actively support the wellbeing of other pupils.

- Pupils behave consistently well, demonstrating high levels of self-control and consistently positive attitudes to their education. If pupils struggle with this, the school takes intelligent, fair and highly effective action to support them to succeed in their education.

(Ofsted, 2019a, p56)

EVIDENCE

Demonstrate evidence to your tutor/mentor of:

- a welcoming physical environment which has a positive effect on pupils' well-being;
- your promotion of 'a thirst for knowledge and understanding' and 'a love of learning' among your pupils;
- a display of rules and/or routines which you expect from pupils;
- your good working knowledge of the school's behaviour policy;
- the effective use of praise with pupils;
- your effective use of (one of) the school's sanctions, if appropriate;
- examples of where you have had an impact on behaviour beyond your own classroom, for example with pupils at breaktimes.

STANDARD 7: MANAGE BEHAVIOUR EFFECTIVELY TO ENSURE A GOOD AND SAFE LEARNING ENVIRONMENT

Have I met Standard 7?

- I have made use of relevant school policies, such as the school's behaviour policy, to secure appropriate learning behaviours.

- I have used a full range of rewards and sanctions fairly and consistently as well as using praise appropriately.

- I have communicated in ways that demonstrate respect for others.

- I have employed a range of strategies to secure effective learning behaviours including self-control and independent learning, so that all learners can make progress.

- I have established and maintained effective relationships with learners.

- I have ensured that learners know the boundaries of acceptable behaviour and understand the consequences of their actions.

- I have minimised the impact of the negative behaviours of some learners on teaching, and on the learning of others.

- I have used different organisational strategies to support individuals and groups effectively.

- I understand the link between learners' behaviour and their involvement and engagement with a lesson.

- I have used high-quality teaching resources to engage and involve learners and help to maintain positive learning behaviours.

- I have worked with colleagues across the wider school to establish a purposeful learning environment, securing appropriate learning behaviours and effective progress.

- I have set realistic targets for learners, and involved them fully in every aspect of learning.

- I recognise and consider the specific needs of individuals and groups of learners.

8

FULFIL WIDER PROFESSIONAL RESPONSIBILITIES

8   A teacher must: fulfil wider professional responsibilities

A   make a positive contribution to the wider life and ethos of the school

B   develop effective professional relationships with colleagues, knowing how and when to draw on advice and specialist support

C   deploy support staff effectively

D   take responsibility for improving teaching through appropriate professional development, responding to advice and feedback from colleagues

E   communicate effectively with parents with regard to pupils' achievements and well-being.

(DfE, 2012a, p9)

——— COMMENTARY ———

A well-respected book about schooling, published in the 1970s, was titled *Fifteen Thousand Hours* (Rutter *et al*., 1979). This was approximately the amount of time that the average child between the ages of 5 and 16 spent in school. A quick bit of

(Continued)

(Continued)

maths suggests this hasn't changed much over the decades! Most of those hours are spent by pupils in classrooms, for which teachers have a lead responsibility. This Standard reminds teachers that their professional role is not confined to the classroom but extends more widely. Many experienced practitioners would at once say that there is as much enjoyment and fulfilment to be had in the wider school context as there is amid the buzz of the classroom.

Standard 8 usefully rounds off Part 1 of the Teachers' Standards, in some ways both echoing the Preamble and serving as a preface to Part 2: Personal and Professional Conduct.

In amplifying the scope of the Standard 8 heading, there are five stated areas for teachers to focus upon.

A   Schools are busy, diverse and interesting places to work, whether it be a small rural primary school or a large urban secondary comprehensive. Each has its own character and personalities, its ways of doing business, history, traditions, quirks and future planning. It is not difficult therefore to find real fulfilment in contributing to the wider life of the school and shaping its ethos. Volunteering to accompany pupils on school journeys, taking sports teams, running a drama or IT or library club, leading maths or literacy booster sessions, taking assemblies, leading staff training – there are many ways in which teachers new to the profession can make a difference to pupils outside classrooms. At the same time you are signalling to the head your professional ambitions to be seen as more than a classroom teacher.

Remember: the whole school community benefits when you share your particular skills and interests.

B   At times, teaching can feel a solitary activity: the teacher on their own with a class of pupils. But this is rare. Good schools' strengths lie in their collegiality, with teaching, support and administrative staff (and governors) always prepared to work together in the best interests of the pupils and fellow staff members. It is important to work hard at establishing positive relationships with close colleagues, drawing on the support of line managers and others with particular expertise, for example special educational needs colleagues, speech therapists, learning mentors. Trainee teachers will have a school-based tutor, and it is reasonable to look to this person to help you sort any teething problems you encounter in your first few months in a school.

A confident leadership team will also take advantage of your 'fresh eyes', and while the eyes are still fresh, ask you if you might suggest any ways in which the school could improve its routines and systems.

C   Depending on your school setting and the age range you teach, you may well have regular support in your classroom from teaching/learning assistants. It is a feature of best early years' practice that teachers, support staff and nursery nurses plan learning activities together; at times in those classrooms it is difficult for a casual observer to say who is the teacher and who is the support member. Through primary school, most class teachers will have some kind of other adult presence, and it is the teacher's key responsibility to ensure that additional support is effectively deployed. This may be designated work with a child with special educational needs, or it may be leading a guided reading group or a maths extension session, and this may take place within the classroom or in a neighbouring space. The teacher retains overall responsibility for the quality of the intervention work and for monitoring pupils' progress.

In a secondary context, teachers may also expect to have in their classrooms colleagues supporting pupils with special educational needs, or it may be that the class has a learning/behaviour mentor accompanying designated pupils. For subject specialists in a number of practical subjects, technicians often work alongside pupils – here again, it is the teacher's role to ensure that deployment is well planned and purposeful. Remember: it is important that support staff are well led by classroom teachers in order that their impact on pupils is significant and good value for money is demonstrated.

D   This point opens with a trenchant phrase: 'take responsibility for'. For the new entrant to the profession, there is a particular imperative to learn quickly, whether in relation to developing knowledge of statutory assessment or in building classroom management skills. In a school you soon learn who are the 'go-to' teachers, those whom you can readily approach for advice and encouragement. It is important to seek out feedback, formal and informal, to try out new ways of doing and to respond to advice as appropriate. To echo a point above: it is trust and mutual respect which leads to genuine collegiality, in any work setting. You learn quickly, and perhaps by trial and error, whose fine judgement you can trust and whose good practice you hope will shape your own.

Schools are places of learning, not only for the pupils but also for the staff. It is vital that teachers avail themselves of purposeful continuous professional development. This can be school-based, led by teachers who are expert in, say, working with higher attaining pupils or managing group work in classrooms. And trainee teachers will usually have some kind of induction programme in their first year, covering a range of relevant topics. Equally, online programmes, courses, conferences and study opportunities beyond the school can provide an invaluable way to stay fresh and keep up-to-date as a teacher. (The Appendix offers a list of titles to extend your horizons.)

(Continued)

(Continued)

E Many schools in their prospectuses make explicit the pivotal triangle of communication and relationships between teachers, pupils and parents. That three-way partnership is vital to a school's overall well-being. The school has a core responsibility to communicate effectively with parents: to communicate regularly and in a way that is accessible to all parents. In working with parents, teachers usually operate within an overall framework or protocol set down by the school to prevent misunderstandings and unrealistic expectations. And of course the primary setting, within which parents meet each other at the school gate and are often in classrooms as volunteers, is a different beast from the inevitably more distant secondary school where alternative ways of working with parents need to operate.

Whatever systems and timetables are in place and consistent with school policy and practice, it is a teacher's responsibility to ensure that parents are kept well informed of their children's achievements and well-being, through regular and clear communication.

REFLECTIONS

1. What has drawn you into the teaching profession? Are you as excited by what you can contribute to the school as a whole as by the buzz of the classroom?

2. What particular skills, expertise and interests will you take to any school you work in?

3. Which staff with specialist knowledge have you gone to for advice? Were you able to act on that advice?

4. As a 'fresh pair of eyes' on your school, what thoughts are you presenting to the leadership team about what works well and what could be improved in the school?

5. What good examples have you observed of support staff in classrooms being well deployed and having a strong learning impact on pupils?

6. How have you harnessed effectively any support staff you have worked with? What planning documents and materials did you provide for them? What expectations did you set out to ensure high impact on pupils' learning?

7. What is the quality of the induction programme in your school?

8. What are its strengths and how are you helping to shape and improve its contents? What wider reading or useful websites for classroom use have you suggested to colleagues?

9. What are the characteristics of the 'go-to' teachers in your school?

10. Do you have a clear understanding of the school's expectations of how you should communicate with parents? What training needs do you have in this area?

EVIDENCE

Demonstrate evidence to your tutor/mentor of:

*   your knowledge of the wider life of the school you are teaching in, e.g. its traditions, extra-curricular strengths, governors' involvement, ethos, etc.;
*   advice and feedback you have received which has helped improve your classroom practice;
*   lesson plans which demonstrate your skilful deployment of teaching assistants or other adults;
*   contributions you have made to school-based in-service training;
*   current wider reading and (perhaps) action research which is informing your practice;
*   successes you have enjoyed in communicating with parents.

STANDARD 8: FULFIL WIDER PROFESSIONAL RESPONSIBILITIES

Have I met Standard 8?

- I have reflected on the contributions I make to the wider life and ethos of the school and what impact these have.

- I have sought guidance and support from, and communicate positively and effectively with, colleagues and other professionals.

- I have established collaborative working relationships with colleagues within and outside the classroom.

- I understand how my role relates to that of other colleagues in school and other support professionals.

- I am able to draw on the expertise of other adults in the classroom.

- I have contributed to planning when working with others - for example, teaching assistants and peers.

- I have engaged with colleagues in the reflection on and discussion of school practice and how to develop it further.

- I am able to brief colleagues sufficiently about the expectations of learners' progress.

- I have monitored the impact of colleagues' work and provided them with positive and constructive feedback.

- I am able to identify and reflect on my main strengths and achievements and on the knowledge, skills and expertise I have developed.

- I am able to critically appraise and justify my own and others' practice in the light of innovation and develop through the innovations of others.

- I have sought opportunities to engage in collaborative planning and teaching.

- I am open to advice and feedback from others, responding positively to constructive criticism in order to develop my professional practice.

- I am able to articulate the benefits of engaging with others, including parents and carers, in supporting learning and teaching, and raising attainment levels.

- I demonstrate sensitivity - for example, to ethnic, cultural and religious factors - when communicating with parents.

9
PERSONAL AND PROFESSIONAL CONDUCT

PART TWO: PERSONAL AND PROFESSIONAL CONDUCT

A teacher is expected to demonstrate consistently high standards of personal and professional conduct. The following statements define the behaviour and attitudes which set the required standard for conduct throughout a teacher's career.

A   Teachers uphold public trust in the profession and maintain high standards of ethics and behaviour, within and outside school, by:

- treating pupils with dignity, building relationships rooted in mutual respect and at all times observing proper boundaries appropriate to a teacher's professional position

- having regard for the need to safeguard pupils' well-being, in accordance with statutory provisions

- showing tolerance of and respect for the rights of others

- not undermining fundamental British values, including democracy, the rule of law, individual liberty and mutual respect, and tolerance of those with different faiths and beliefs

- ensuring that personal beliefs are not expressed in ways which exploit pupils' vulnerability or might lead them to break the law

B   Teachers must have proper and professional regard for the ethos, policies and practices of the school in which they teach, and maintain high standards in their own attendance and punctuality

C   Teachers must have an understanding of, and always act within, the statutory frameworks which set out their professional duties and responsibilities.

(DfE, 2012a, p10)

——— COMMENTARY ———

By way of background, in the accompanying DfE notes on the Teachers' Standards , it is made clear that Part 2 of the document replaces the General Teaching Council for England's *Code of Conduct and Practice for Registered Teachers* which ceased to have effect on 1 September 2012.

The DfE notes also make clear that in order to meet the Standards, a trainee or teacher will need to demonstrate that 'their practice is consistent with the definition set out in the Preamble, and that they have met the standards in both Part 1 and Part 2' (DfE, 2012a, para. 12, p4).

The Preamble (see p1) and Part 2 should be read together. They provide a bedrock for the profession. Teachers should scrutinise carefully what is being expected of them, whether in their first or thirtieth year of teaching, and reflect thoughtfully on the carefully chosen words and phrases set out above. When in doubt about a particular situation - for example, about the use of social media or an issue of 'confidentiality' - do seek the advice of an experienced colleague.

ADVICE ON YOUR ONLINE PROFILE AND SOCIAL MEDIA ACTIVITY

Teachers need to be aware of the content of their online profile and should recognise that materials 'posted' can be seen by others, including a wider group of people other than those 'befriended' on social media. Consequently, it is vital that teachers who use social media apply strong privacy settings and think carefully about the way they use technology. Although social media can be an effective way to develop supportive networks, allowing for the exchange information, ideas and knowledge, there have been cases of teachers being subjected to disciplinary action because unsuitable materials have been posted or shared online. Table 9.1 details the actions you can take to protect your online reputation.

Table 9.1 Actions that you can take to protect your online reputation

• Ensuring that I use appropriate language
• Not posting offensive information about others or myself (this includes comments, pictures or videos)
• Not discussing pupils, colleagues or parents online
• Respecting the views of others
• Familiarising myself with the school's 'IT acceptable use' policy and abiding by the requirements (e.g. avoiding the use of personal emails and social media when connected to my school's Wi-Fi network and not using work emails for personal use)
• Not allowing others to use my work equipment
• Ensuring that all devices are password protected
• Not leaving my computer 'unlocked' when I move away from it
• Not befriending any students or parents on social media
• Not accepting friend requests from people I do not know
• Reviewing my privacy settings and customising who can see my posts
• Not providing my personal phone number to pupils or parents (use the school mobile for school trips)
• Not joining online groups that are radical or offensive to others
• Not joining groups that pupils have signed up to out of school
• Not publishing pictures or videos without consent from the 'author'
• Not using inappropriate nicknames
• Looking online periodically so that I am aware of what others are viewing

In summary, before posting materials online, stop and ask yourself:

1.   Might this reflect poorly on me, the school or the teaching profession?

2.   Am I confident that the comment (or other media) if accessed by others (e.g. colleagues or parents) would be considered appropriate?

If the answer to the questions is 'no' then do not post the material. There are, however, occasions when others associated with you may post information that is offensive to you and could impact upon your professional career. Examples are shown below in Table 9.2.

Table 9.2 The impact of others on a teacher's online profile

• Students or parents discussing your work in a negative way
• Other people adding inappropriate tagging or comments that are visible on your social media
• Doctored content about you
• Hackers using your post inappropriately
• Family and friends being unsure of how they can protect your online reputation

If hurtful information is posted online by a pupil or parents it is important that you make copies of the offensive content and take them to your headteacher. Your headteacher must act on cyberbullying. Similarly, if your account has been hacked, it is important that your school knows so that passwords can be re-set and actions taken to protect the school's systems.

For further information about keeping safe online, look at the following websites:

http://www.gtcs.org.uk/web/FILES/teacher-regulation/professional-guidance-ecomms-social-media.pdf

https://www.saferinternet.org.uk/our-helplines

https://www.childnet.com/downloads/Social-Media-Guide-teachers-and-support-staff.pdf

REFLECTIONS

1. 'At all times observing proper boundaries appropriate to a teacher's professional position.'

What does that mean in practice for you, as a new entrant into the profession? Think ahead. What situations might arise where you have to make prompt judgements about what to do or not do in order to observe proper boundaries?

2. What does the term 'safeguarding' mean to you? Do you have a secure working understanding of the school's safeguarding procedures and your responsibilities within them? Rehearse your understanding with an experienced colleague.

3. In what kind of situations might you find yourself having to balance the rights of different pupils? Think about some possible scenarios and your proposed actions. Again, talk these through with a colleague who has a very good knowledge of the pupils and families at your school.

4. 'Not undermining fundamental British values, etc.'

The DfE notes indicate that the phrase *fundamental British values is taken from the definition of extremism as articulated in the Prevent Strategy, launched in June 2011* (DfE, 2012a, p5). Discuss with a couple of colleagues how this aspect of expected conduct might arise in your school.

5. Do you have any strongly held beliefs, for example with regard to politics, religion or social mores? How do you make sure that in the classroom these beliefs do not 'exploit pupils' vulnerability'?

6. Teachers must act within statutory frameworks. The DfE notes state: *Statutory frameworks includes all legal requirements ... The term also covers the professional duties of teachers as set out in the statutory School Teachers' Pay and Conditions Document.* Familiarise yourself with the most recent Pay and Conditions document to see how what is set out there complements the Teachers' Standards (DfE, 2012b).

Looking back through Part 2 of the Teachers' Standards, which aspects of conduct do you think are going to provide you with the greatest challenges in your early months and years of teaching?

INTERLUDE: VISITING A YEAR 10 CLASSROOM

Read through the following questions which aim to help you reflect on and analyse best practice.

(a) When you visit a colleague's upper secondary classroom, use the following questions as a checklist against which you make observations.

(b) At the end of a given week, use the questions to help you reflect on your own best practice and where you might wish to fine-tune your own classroom.

(c) Add your own questions to the checklist as you develop your own skills in lesson observations.

Questions to ask

1. What are your first impressions of the learning environment?
    - Is it light, airy and the right temperature for learning?
    - Does the room celebrate the specialist subject being taught?
    - Does the room celebrate Year 10 work?
    - How do the students react to your presence as a visitor?

2. In what ways does the style of teaching and learning reflect that this is a Year 10 class and not a Year 7 class? (For example, how is furniture configured? Where does the teacher position her/himself?)

3. In the time you are in the room, count the minutes (a) the teacher talks and (b) students converse with a proper focus. Is the teacher working harder than the students?

4. What evidence can you see of Year 10's independent learning skills? If the teacher left the room, would students' focus continue?

5. Are the students teaching? What opportunities are students given to *apply* newly acquired knowledge and skills?

6. Is the level of work appropriate for more able students, irrespective of mixed-ability or setted group? If not, how would you make it more demanding?

7. How has homework led into this lesson? How is homework/further independent study/research following up the lesson?

8. What evidence is there of (a) fun, (b) scholarship, (c) intriguing digressions or (d) the teacher sharing personal enthusiasms?

9. How well does the teacher demonstrate his/her own specialist subject knowledge? Does s/he extend horizons and arouse students' interest?

10. How creatively are book/technology resources harnessed to stimulate students' interest and extend their skills and knowledge?

11. Can you tell from looking at books/folders whether students fully understand syllabus demands ('the story of their learning')? Is there a difference in the quality of note-taking and storage between girls and boys?

12. Are targets for individuals and groups in place? Is marking formative and does it advise students on how they can improve from, say, GCSE grade 7 to grade 8? Do students know what top-quality work in the subject looks like?

13. How is the teaching *deepening* pupils' knowledge and skills?

10

MASTER TEACHER

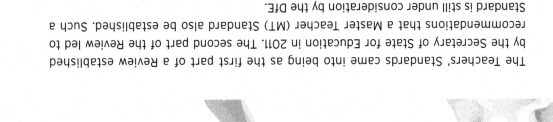

The Teachers' Standards came into being as the first part of a Review established by the Secretary of State for Education in 2011. The second part of the Review led to recommendations that a Master Teacher (MT) Standard also be established. Such a Standard is still under consideration by the DfE.

For those teachers who see themselves developing strongly within the profession, what is set out below is worth reading and reflecting on, whether or not the MT Standard is taken up in some way formally by government and the profession, perhaps through a future Royal College for Teaching.

The MT Standard is rooted in international best practice and what some of the world's most successful school systems expect of their teachers. It presents a focused definition of those teachers who are demonstrating excellent practice, and, in the words of the Review, who have the potential to make the most significant and positive impact *on their pupils, their peers and on the profession as a whole* (DfE, 2011b, p3).

Furthermore, the Standard shows how an excellent teacher, working across the full breadth of the Teachers' Standards, might demonstrate consistently the very best of classroom practice.

For trainee teachers, the Master Teacher narrative descriptions (each of just three paragraphs) might stand as aspirational, a goal ahead to be achieved following a few years of demonstrating consistently excellent practice and making a decisive impact over time on their pupils. For all reflective practitioners, the descriptions could be seen as 'extension expectations' when compared with the main Teachers' Standards.

The MT Standard begins with an introduction, an echo of the Preamble to the main Teachers' Standards. It is followed by five sections which in many ways usefully distil the essence of what it is to be a highly skilled classroom practitioner. The five domains - knowledge, classroom performance, outcomes, environment and ethos, professional context - are commonly to be found in the professional expectations of teachers across the world, including those from Finland, Singapore, the USA, New Zealand, Dubai and Germany.

Following the Master Teacher Standard text below, there is a series of Reflections to help you interrogate the text.

THE MASTER TEACHER STANDARD

This Standard should be read as part of a profile of a Master Teacher who may have his or her own particular strengths in specific areas. Above all, a Master Teacher is someone whose professionalism has come to be seen as an integral part of his or her character.

Master Teachers are excellent teachers, deeply committed to making a difference to the lives of their pupils. The Master Teacher is a self-assured presence in the classroom, who effortlessly captures pupils' imagination.

Although Master Teachers may take on management and other roles in the school, there is no presumption that they will move outside the classroom. They are exceptional practitioners, for whom high levels of performance in the basic Teachers' Standards are taken as given. They are enthusiastic about their specialism or subject(s).[1] They have a strong sense of the significance of what they teach in the context of the whole curriculum and beyond.

A Knowledge

Master Teachers have deep and extensive knowledge of their specialism, going far beyond the set programmes they teach. They have an intrinsic curiosity about their specialism, keep up with developments, and their teaching reflects their own passion and expertise. They respond intelligently and confidently to the unexpected and wide-ranging questions their pupils are encouraged to ask, and they are able to lead discussions and explorations which take pupils beyond the confines of teaching programmes.

They are able to teach their specialism clearly, intelligently and inventively, showing considerable breadth and initiative. They have a keen sense of the most effective and engaging ways of communicating the subject matter to pupils of all abilities and aptitudes.

Master Teachers are reflective and self-critical regarding their own teaching and make critical appraisals of new developments and techniques, which they use judiciously. A thorough understanding of the developmental and social backgrounds of pupils further supports and informs their practice.

B Classroom performance

Master Teachers command the classroom, skilfully leading, encouraging and extending pupils.[2] They have the respect of both pupils and parents. They are at ease in their role, and discipline and dialogue are unselfconscious and effective.

Teaching is motivating, often inspiring, and basic principles are expertly taught. Expectations are challengingly high, realistic, based on sound experience and take into account the abilities of all pupils. The pacing of lessons is well orchestrated and transitions between whole-class teaching, group and individual work are seamless. Questioning and discussion are of a high order, relevant and at times deep.

Pupils are consistently focused and engaged in their studies and are encouraged effectively to reflect on their own progress. Homework and independent study activities are wisely chosen to extend the range and depth of pupils' knowledge, understanding and acquisition of skills. Master Teachers ensure that high-quality assessment and feedback are consistently prompt, rigorous and constructive. They enable pupils to identify and remedy their misunderstandings and build on their successes. They promote pupils' desire to seek and apply their knowledge further.

C Outcomes

The Master Teacher's meticulous planning and organisation ensure that pupils are well prepared for all forms of assessment. Outcomes achieved by pupils in the context in question are outstanding. They have an awareness of school, national and international benchmarks and examination reports, including data from maintained and independent schools.

Master Teachers have an extensive understanding of and expertise in relevant assessment systems and examinations. They make critical use of data, relating to the prior and current performance of pupils, to underpin and motivate improvement. As a result, pupils understand what they are learning and have a strong grasp of the principles on which the knowledge and capacities in question are based.

Outcomes are also outstanding in a more informal sense. Pupils not only understand what they have been taught and its significance, and are able to deploy

(Continued)

(Continued)

this knowledge critically and analytically, but they are also inspired to go beyond what they have been taught.

D Environment and ethos

The class is one in which pupils feel welcome and valued. There is a stimulating culture of scholarship alongside a sense of mutual respect and good manners. The Master Teacher has an excellent rapport with classes and with individual pupils.

The classroom environment created to support study and activities is an inspirational example of practice, appropriate to the age range or phase. Resources, including books and IT, are well chosen and stimulating, contributing significantly to progress in lessons. Resources excite, extend and support different abilities, interests and aptitudes.

In classrooms for younger pupils, visual stimuli arising from children's own work offer powerful models to which other children can aspire. In classrooms for older pupils, scholarship is also evident in the classroom surroundings. Displays often reflect contemporary events and a breadth of subject matter which extend beyond the subject under study.

E Professional context

Master Teachers are highly regarded by colleagues who want to learn from them. They willingly play a role in the development of school policies and in the professional life of the school. They work in collaboration with colleagues on pastoral and wider pupil-related matters, giving advice as appropriate. They engage with and contribute to professional networks beyond the school.

They are analytical in evaluating and developing their own craft and knowledge, making full use of continuing professional development and appropriate research. They recognise the vital importance of out-of-school and extra-curricular activities, both academically and personally, and play a leading role here and in the wider life of the school.

Master Teachers are open in the giving and receiving of professional advice, which may include coaching or mentoring colleagues and less-experienced teachers. They work to significant effect with other adults in ensuring high-quality education for the pupils they serve.

Notes

1. References to 'specialism' should be taken to mean 'subject(s) or specialisms'.
2. 'Classroom' should be read as extending to all other environments in which Master Teachers work.

(DfE, 2011b, pp9–11)

REFLECTIONS

1. What are your thoughts on the idea of a Master Teacher Standard? Is it useful for the profession to have a narrative describing excellent practice?

2. Do you think the Introduction to the MT Standard (p62) builds constructively on the Preamble to the main Teachers' Standards? Would you wish to see anything else added?

3. What do you think of the descriptions in the 'Knowledge' section? In what ways are these a more demanding set of expectations than is to be found in Teachers' Standard 3?

4. In the 'Classroom Performance' section, the bar is set high: 'command' in the classroom; 'inspiring' teaching; expectations 'challengingly high'; and assessment and feedback are 'consistently prompt, rigorous and constructive'. What examples have you seen in classrooms of some or all of the points listed? Where do your emerging strengths lie?

5. While Teachers' Standard 2 is headed 'Progress and Outcomes', the MT Standard simply states 'Outcomes', a reflection of international best practice. Is it important to make the notion of 'progress' explicit or not? Why, or why not?

6. The MT Standard is short and pithy by its nature and design. Try drafting a fourth paragraph to add to the 'Environment and Ethos' section, directly linked to the age range you are teaching.

7. How important in your view is the final section 'Professional Context'? Is it your experience that teachers generally see themselves occupying this wider, outward-facing professional role?

8. What else do experienced colleagues do which you find highly effective with pupils and professionally exciting, and which might be added to a revised set of Master Teacher Standards?

11

OFSTED'S EVALUATION OF THE QUALITY OF EDUCATION

OFSTED SCHOOL INSPECTION HANDBOOK

The inspection for the 'quality of education' judgement is structured to ensure that inspectors are able to gather evidence of how well a school is positioned to deliver a high-quality education for its pupils. The inspection will focus on gathering first-hand evidence from lessons, talking to individual teachers and pupils, and looking at pupils' work. The crucial element of the inspection process is the connection between different pieces of evidence. Inspectors will concentrate on gathering evidence that is balanced and connected. The focus will not be on one particular lesson, book or pupil; rather, it will be on the interconnection of all of these pieces of evidence and what they tell inspectors and leaders about whether pupils are learning the curriculum and making progress in the sense of knowing more, remembering more and being able to do more.

One element of the inspection approach will be visits to lessons. The lead inspector will invite the headteacher, curriculum leaders and other leaders to take part in joint visits to lessons. Inspectors will not observe a random sample of lessons; instead, they will connect lesson visits to other evidence: discussions with curriculum leaders, teachers and pupils, and work scrutiny. Inspectors will visit several lessons in the same subject, including lessons to different year groups. Lesson visits are not about evaluating individual teachers or their teaching so there will be no grading of the teaching observed by inspectors. Instead, inspectors will view lessons across a faculty, department, subject, key stage or year group and then aggregate insights in order to evaluate the school's curriculum intentions.

In summary, lesson visits are primarily useful for gathering evidence about how lessons contribute to the quality of education, for example, providing evidence about how well the curriculum is implemented. They do this by looking at what is going on in lessons for one or more subjects or themes and triangulating this with evidence collected through discussions with the staff and pupils involved, and scrutinising the pupils' work.

(Ofsted, 2019a, pp26-7)

———— INTENT, IMPLEMENTATION AND IMPACT ————

Inspectors will consider the extent to which the school's curriculum sets out the knowledge and skills that pupils will gain at each stage (we call this '**intent**'). They will also consider the way that the curriculum developed or adopted by the school is taught and assessed in order to support pupils to build their knowledge and to apply that knowledge as skills (we call this '**implementation**'). Finally, inspectors will consider the outcomes that pupils achieve as a result of the education they have received (we call this '**impact**').

(Ofsted, 2019a, p41, original emphasis)

GRADE DESCRIPTORS – QUALITY OF EDUCATION IN THE SCHOOL

Note: These descriptors should not be used as a checklist. They must be applied adopting a 'best fit' approach that relies on the professional judgement of the inspection team.

Outstanding (1)

- The school meets **all** the criteria for a good quality of education **securely** and **consistently**.

- The quality of education provided is **exceptional**.

In addition, the following apply.

- The school's curriculum intent and implementation are embedded securely and consistently across the school. It is evident from what teachers do that they have a firm and common understanding of the school's curriculum intent and what it means for their practice. Across all parts of the school, series of lessons contribute well to delivering the curriculum intent.

- The work given to pupils, over time and across the school, consistently matches the aims of the curriculum. It is coherently planned and sequenced towards cumulatively sufficient knowledge and skills for future learning and employment.

- Pupils' work across the curriculum is consistently of a high quality.

- Pupils consistently achieve highly, particularly the most disadvantaged. Pupils with SEND achieve exceptionally well.

Good (2)

Intent

- Leaders adopt or construct a curriculum that is ambitious and designed to give all pupils, particularly disadvantaged pupils and including pupils with SEND, the knowledge and cultural capital they need to succeed in life. This is either the national curriculum or a curriculum of comparable breadth and ambition.

- The school's curriculum is coherently planned and sequenced towards cumulatively sufficient knowledge and skills for future learning and employment.

- The curriculum is successfully adapted, designed or developed to be ambitious and meet the needs of pupils with SEND, developing their knowledge, skills and abilities to apply what they know and can do with increasing fluency and independence.

- Pupils study the full curriculum; it is not narrowed. In primary schools, a broad range of subjects (exemplified by the national curriculum) is taught in key stage 2 throughout each and all of Years 3 to 6. In secondary schools, the school teaches a broad range of subjects (exemplified by the national curriculum) throughout Years 7 to 9. The school's aim is to have the English Baccalaureate (EBacc) at the heart of its curriculum, in line with the DfE's ambition, and good progress has been made towards this ambition.

Implementation

- Teachers have good knowledge of the subject(s) and courses they teach. Leaders provide effective support for those teaching outside their main areas of expertise.

- Teachers present subject matter clearly, promoting appropriate discussion about the subject matter being taught. They check pupils' understanding systematically, identify misconceptions accurately and provide clear, direct feedback. In so doing, they respond and adapt their teaching as necessary without unnecessarily elaborate or individualised approaches.

- Over the course of study, teaching is designed to help pupils to remember long term the content they have been taught and to integrate new knowledge into larger ideas.

- Teachers and leaders use assessment well - for example, to help pupils embed and use knowledge fluently, or to check understanding and inform teaching. Leaders understand the limitations of assessment and do not use it in a way that creates unnecessary burdens on staff or pupils.

- Teachers create an environment that focuses on pupils. The textbooks and other teaching materials that teachers select - in a way that does not create unnecessary workload for staff - reflect the school's ambitious intentions for the course of study. These materials clearly support the intent of a coherently planned curriculum, sequenced towards cumulatively sufficient knowledge and skills for future learning and employment.

- The work given to pupils is demanding and matches the aims of the curriculum in being coherently planned and sequenced towards cumulatively sufficient knowledge.

- Reading is prioritised to allow pupils to access the full curriculum offer.

- A rigorous and sequential approach to the reading curriculum develops pupils' fluency, confidence and enjoyment in reading. At all stages, reading attainment is assessed and gaps are addressed quickly and effectively for all pupils. Reading books connect closely to the phonics knowledge pupils are taught when they are learning to read.

- The sharp focus on ensuring that younger children gain phonics knowledge and language comprehension necessary to read, and the skills to communicate, gives them the foundations for future learning.

- Teachers ensure that their own speaking, listening, writing and reading of English support pupils in developing their language and vocabulary well.

Impact

- Pupils develop detailed knowledge and skills across the curriculum and, as a result, achieve well. This is reflected in results from national tests and examinations that meet government expectations, or in the qualifications obtained.

- Pupils are ready for the next stage of education, employment or training. They have the knowledge and skills they need and, where relevant, they gain qualifications that allow them to go on to destinations that meet their interests and aspirations and the intention of their course of study. Pupils with SEND achieve the best possible outcomes.

- Pupils' work across the curriculum is of good quality.

- Pupils read widely and often, with fluency and comprehension appropriate to their age. They are able to apply mathematical knowledge, concepts and procedures appropriately for their age.

Requires improvement (3)

- The quality of education provided by the school is not good.

Inadequate (4)

The quality of education is likely to be inadequate if any one of the following applies.

- The school's curriculum has little or no structure or coherence, and leaders have not appropriately considered sequencing. Pupils experience a jumbled, disconnected series of lessons that do not build their knowledge, skills or understanding.

- The pupils' experiences in lessons contribute weakly to their learning of the intended curriculum.

- The range of subjects is narrow and does not prepare pupils for the opportunities, responsibilities and experiences of life in modern Britain.

- Pupils cannot communicate, read, write or apply mathematics sufficiently well for their age and are therefore unable to succeed in the next year or stage of education, or in training or employment. (This does not apply for some pupils with SEND.)

- The progress that disadvantaged pupils make is consistently well below that of other pupils nationally and shows little or no improvement.

- Expectations of pupils with SEND are low, and their needs are not accurately identified, assessed or met.

- Pupils have not attained the qualifications appropriate for them to progress to their next stages of education, training or employment.

(Ofsted, 2019a, pp49-52, original emphasis)

KEY TERMS AND CONCEPTS

The way in which the curriculum is designed and implemeted should enable children to recall facts and to develop key skills. The education inspection framework (EIF) is underpinned by a wealth of research and there are key terms and concepts that teachers should be aware of in order to help them to deliver a curriculum that enables children to remember key concepts.

Spaced learning

Learning can be defined as a change in long-term memory. It is, therefore, important that teachers use approaches that help learners integrate new knowledge into the long-term memory and help them to make connections. Spaced or distributed practice is an approach whereby knowledge is rehearsed for short bursts of time, over a long period of time and is deemed to be more effective than intensive learning for a shorter period of time. It is, therefore, good practice to block learning and repeat practice over time, as this leads to better long-term retention of knowledge (Rohrer, 2012; Rawson and Kintsch, 2005, cited in Ofsted, 2019b).

Retrieval

Retrieval practice involves recalling something that has been previously learned and recalling it again. Retrieval practice needs to occur a reasonable time after the topic has been initially taught and may take the form of testing knowledge, by the teacher or through pupil self-testing. It is important that feedback on accuracy is provided either by the teacher or by the pupil checking accuracy for themselves.

Elaboration

Elaboration is defined as describing and explaining something learned to others in some detail. Ideally, this involves making connections among ideas and connecting the material to one's memory and experiences. It can also be useful for learners to ask themselves or each other questions that require making connections between ideas or explaining them.

Dual coding

In presenting material, teachers can make use of dual coding. Dual coding theory suggests that representing information both visually and verbally enhances learning and retrieval from memory. The principle underlying this is that visual and verbal information are processed through different channels in the brain, creating separate representations for information processed in each channel (Paivio, 1990; Clark and Paivio, 1991, cited in Ofsted, 2019b).

Cognitive load

An important contribution to learning science is made by cognitive load theory (CLT). CLT is concerned with the architecture of memory and the brain, and in particular the capacity of the short-term memory to process information. The long-term memory consists of a range of schemata, which are complex structures that link knowledge and create meaning and which are built up over time. Learning is essentially about changing those schemata, through acquiring knowledge and making connections with different schemata. However, before entering long-term memory and developing schemata, information must first be processed by the short-term or working memory.

(Ofsted, 2019b)

─────────── **COMMENTARY** ───────────

Teachers across England are familiar with the work of Ofsted and its school inspectors. Since its creation in 1992, Ofsted has operated various inspection frameworks. In the 2019 Framework for Inspection, schools are judged on a four-point scale under five principal headings:

- Overall effectiveness
- Quality of education
- Behaviour and attitudes
- Personal development
- Leadership and management

(Provision for the early years and for the sixth form is also graded. Teachers involved in either of these phases should read the specific Ofsted criteria to inform their practice.)

The Teachers' Standards set out expectations which are intended to lead to good practice being the norm across the country. As you read over the Standards and compare what Ofsted outlines above in relation to the quality of education, you should come across much common ground. Of course, teachers should have a secure understanding of the whole inspection framework, not just that relating to the quality of education outcomes.

There is a coming together in the two documents which spells out roundly just how important it is that teachers everywhere deliver the curricluum in a way that will genuinely get the best from every individual pupil, no matter which classroom she or he is in.

REFLECTIONS

1. Look at a curriculum plan for the school, how is the curriculum sequenced? Are there blocks of work? How is the work sequenced so that children can recall leaning? What is the rationale behind/underpinning the planning?

2. Run through Ofsted's definitions of good provision. Match up each of the bullet points with a corresponding statement in the Teachers' Standards. Are there any aspects which do not readily correspond?

3. School inspection frameworks in different parts of the world rely on a stock of comparative adjectives and adverbs to indicate different levels of competency and progression. Pick out (a) the adjectives and (b) the adverbs that signal good practices.

4. In your own classroom, how can you secure consistently 'good' practice? Which aspects need particular focus?

5. Seek out opportunities to work with a subject leader to understand:

    a. what the curriculum aims are for the subject area, including the knowledge and understanding to be gained at each year group or key stage (intent)

    b. how the subject is implemented so that pupils remember long term the content they have been taught

    c. how the subject is sequenced to develop understanding

    d. how the curriculum area is monitored in terms of the knowledge and understanding pupils have gained against expectations (impact)

    e. how gaps and overlaps are identified.

12
DELIVERING QUALITY EDUCATION

KEY MESSAGES FROM THE CHIEF INSPECTOR'S REPORT AND THE EDUCATION INSPECTION FRAMEWORK

THE EDUCATION INSPECTION FRAMEWORK (EIF)

The new EIF places more emphasis on assessing whether a school has a well-designed curriculum that is ambitious and has high expectations for all learners. In the first phase of Ofsted's curriculum research project, it found that school leaders were focused on increasing performance measures and teaching to the test. In addition to this, 'narrowing the curriculum' was common practice (Ofsted, 2020a). The following case study by Ofsted highlights the impact of a restrictive curriculum on outcomes for pupils.

—————— CASE STUDY ——————

Our curriculum research this year showed that, in a number of primary schools, headteachers had decided to focus on English and mathematics over other subjects, including science. This was often done explicitly to improve test results in English and mathematics. We saw that both quantity and quality of science teaching were reduced. In these schools, pupils were often given little access to science content. Little consideration was given to developing scientific concepts and skills and the vocabulary that comes with being taught science. The deprioritisation

(Continued)

(Continued)

of primary science by schools may be part of the reason why in the otherwise generally encouraging set of PISA outcomes last year, science showed a further decline. The children who took PISA science tests in 2015 and 2018 are the first who did not take the key stage 2 science test at primary school. We understand the incentives that have led many primary schools to limit science teaching, and the difficulties of ensuring that teachers themselves have sufficient scientific knowledge to teach it well. However, there is enough room in the timetable to give children plenty of time for English and mathematics at the same time as building their knowledge in science. We are pleased that the DfE is planning to work with a small number of schools in the development of complete curriculum programmes for science at key stage 2. More generally, this erosion shows what can happen when neither inspection nor testing look below the surface at subject level, and the importance of the curriculum focus in our new framework.

(Ofsted, 2020a, page 9)

Consequently, the aim of the EIF is to ensure that children are exposed to a broad and balanced education. The rationale for this is to build children's capital so that they have opportunities to 'discover the joys of langauges, art, music, drama and humanities' (Ofsted, 2020b). This aligns with Bourdieu's concept of 'capital' (referring to economic, cultural and social resources that an individual has). If children have the 'right sort' of capital, they are better able to 'get on' in life (Archer *et al*, 2015). For example, if children are not read to, rarely or never taken to the museums, art galleries, the beach, woodlands or zoos at the weekend, then they are likely to have a low capital. It is essential that these children have a proper, substantial and broad education so that they may develop their talents in different subject areas and this may help to improve their life chances. Ofsted (2020b) reports that, as a country, we could lose talent, imagination and the scholars of the future if we restrict their education (Ofsted, 2020b). Ofsted (2020a) is concerned that some providers are failing to act with integrity or focus on what really matters. As a result, some children, particularly the most disadvantaged, are not being well prepared for adult life.

THE CURRICULUM

The strength of a school is measured by how well it educates all children. The quality of education is assessed through Intent, Implementation and Impact (see Chapter 11). In schools that score highly on the curriculum indicators the following were in place:

- the curriculum was at least as ambitious as the national curriculum

- subject leaders had clear roles and good subject knowledge

- there was effective curriculum planning in all subjects

- as many pupils as possible had access to a rich and broad curriculum

- the school's curriculum had sufficient depth and coverage of knowledge, including a well-thought-out model of progression and sequencing.

Ofsted (2020a, p10)

DEEP DIVES

Ofsted inspects the quality of education by starting with a top-level view of the curriculum and testing this out with 'deep dives' into individual subjects. These include:

- discussions with senior leaders

- discussions with curriculum leaders

- visits to a connected sample of lessons

- discussions with teachers

- discussions with learners

- scrutiny of learners' work ...

The aim is to assess the planning and sequencing of the curriculum and how this is being implemented in the classroom.

(Ofsted, 2020a, p11)

WHAT IS MY ROLE DURING A 'DEEP DIVE'?

A 'deep dive' is an approach to gain a deeper understanding of a school's curriculum and to find out what the school intends for the children to learn and when they will learn it. Conversations with staff and children, scrutiny of work and observations of lessons enable inspectors to collect a wide range of evidence so that they are able to make an accurate judgement about the quality of education.

Discussions with senior leaders

The inspection will begin with a telephone conversation with senior leaders of the school during which the school's curriculum aims, teaching approaches, rationale, coverage, evidence of progression and long-term plans are shared. When the Ofsted team arrives at school it will triangulate the data from the telephone conversation by meeting with subject leads, observing teaching, having discussions with teachers and children and scrutinising books. All members of staff will be key to the inspection process and it is important that you are aware of the curriculum aims, signature pedagogy and the progression and sequencing of learning in each subject area. The number of subjects chosen for a 'deep dive', will depend upon the size of the school and the length of the inspection. Reading will always be a focus and the other subjects may be selected if they have been highlighted as a strength of the school or if the subject area is a priority for development.

Discussions with a subject lead

Ofsted will talk about the chosen 'deep dive' subject (or subjects) with the appropriate subject lead(s). The interview will focus on how the subject has been planned across the school and the rationale for this. It will be interested in how children learn skills and concepts in the subject area. It is likely that the subject lead will be asked questions about signature pedagogy, how the curriculum is designed so that there is coverage and progression throughout the school and links to other subject areas. The subject leader may also be asked questions based upon the inspector's visits to lessons and scrutiny of work.

Visits to a connected sample of lessons

Having spoken with the senior leaders and the subject leaders, Ofsted inspectors will have a well-developed understanding of the rationale, aims and approach for the 'deep dive' subject area. They will then visit lessons to see if what is happening in lessons matches this. For example, if the subject lead asserts that enquiry is a key pedagogical approach, then Ofsted will want to see if this is the case and will want to know how the lessons build on prior learning and fit into the sequence of lessons so that there is depth of learning.

Discussions with teachers

Having observed a lesson, Ofsted will want to know how the class teacher plans sequences of learning, so that children learn the key skills and knowledge in the subject area. It may wish to know how well the teachers build upon prior learning and are aware of how they are preparing learners for the next steps. It may ask what the teacher does if a child missed a lesson or what actions are taken if a child is finding the work challenging.

Discussions with children

Discussions with children will provide evidence of how well the curriculum content is learned and retained. Inspectors will want to talk to a cross-section of children, including those whom they have seen in lessons and whose work they have scrutinised.

Children may be asked to recap on their learning in the previous year. Inspectors will also listen to children read and may discuss the learning of reading with the children.

Scrutiny of learners' work

To provide a broad picture of children's learning Ofsted may scrutinise children's work. It may focus on how misconceptions have been addressed so that they do not hinder future learning; the clarity of Learning Intentions and Success Criteria and possibly use of subject-specific language.

REFLECTIONS

1. Look afresh at a sequence of recent lesson plans for a subject. How does the sequence of lessons support children to learn new knowledge and skills? How closely does this sequence align to the National Curriculum and how often do you build in opportunities to revist objectives? How do your questions promote learning and enquiry?

2. Which techniques do you deploy well to ensure that you check pupils' learning at the right intervals in a lesson? What do you find are the most effective ways in lessons of summing up newly acquired knowledge and skills so that pupils *deepen* their learning?

3. Look at the curriculum plan for a subject area and consider how this is planned and sequenced to support depth of learning. What skills and knowledge will a child learn from their first to final year in the school? How do you know what is happening in that subject across the school? How does assessment feed into learning?

4. Which techniques have you developed to ensure pupils use and enjoy correct subject-specific vocabulary, whether in science, mathematics or design? How have you followed this up with meaningful homework?

5. In Amanda Spielman's speech (Ofsted, 2020b), she identifies that children should have a broad and balanced curriculum so that they may develop their talents in different subject areas to help improve their life chances. How would you build pupil's 'capital' by enriching the curriculum?

Note: Gather together your reflections above, as necessary, to provide written portfolio evidence of meeting the Teachers' Standards.

13

EXTENDING YOUR PRACTICE TO MEET THE TEACHERS' STANDARDS

This chapter covers a number of the Teachers' Standards. A range of information and checklists is provided. The reader then has a series of questions against which they can usefully judge whether they are meeting the Standards and have the requisite evidence to present.

A. NATIONAL CURRICULUM

Standard 3 expects all teachers to demonstrate secure, relevant subject and curriculum knowledge, lying at the heart of their everyday practice across the 5–16 age range. Many teachers of course will make themselves equally familiar with the knowledge required for effective teaching of the early years and post-16 students.

The 2014 National Curriculum presents both continuity and change in curriculum content, when compared with previous editions. *Programmes of study* and *attainment targets* remain in the vocabulary of planning. *Core* and *foundation* subjects similarly remain as a way of grouping subjects, each including statutory and non-statutory requirements. There is significant emphasis given to English, mathematics and science respectively.

The structure is clearly set out across the four key stages, as follows:

The core aim of the National Curriculum is to provide all pupils with *an introduction to the essential knowledge that they need to be educated citizens. It introduces pupils to the best that has been thought and said and helps engender an appreciation of human creativity and achievement.*

Table 13.1 *Structure of the National Curriculum*

	Key stage 1	Key stage 2	Key stage 3	Key stage 4
Age	5-7	7-11	11-14	14-16
Year groups	1-2	3-6	7-9	10-11
Core subjects:				
English	✓	✓	✓	✓
Mathematics	✓	✓	✓	✓
Science	✓	✓	✓	✓
Foundation subjects:				
Arts and design	✓	✓	✓	
Citizenship			✓	✓
Computing	✓	✓	✓	✓
Design and technology	✓	✓	✓	
Languages		✓	✓	
Geography	✓	✓	✓	
History	✓	✓	✓	
Music	✓	✓	✓	
Physical education	✓	✓	✓	✓

Source: The National Curriculum in England, (DfE September 2013).

Table 13.2 *Statutory teaching of religious education and sex and relationship education*

	Key stage 1	Key stage 2	Key stage 3	Key stage 4
Age	5-7	7-11	11-14	14-16
Year groups	1-2	3-6	7-9	10-11
Religious education	✓	✓	✓	✓
Sex and relationship education			✓	✓

Source: The National Curriculum in England, (DfE September 2013).

Strong cross-curricular themes are:

- Inclusion

- High expectations of every pupil

- Numeracy and mathematics

- Language and literacy.

An assessment regime is not stipulated, with schools free to adapt the familiar system of levels or evolve new systems.

REFLECTIONS AND EVIDENCE

1. From your reading of the programmes of study which you are teaching, are there any particular aspects which require you to do further training, reading or revision of previously learned subject matter? If so, how might your school and colleagues support you with professional development?

2. How do you structure your lesson planning to ensure the cross-curricular themes are included where appropriate? What written records are of value to make?

3. What is your school doing to evolve new systems of assessment beyond the familiar National Curriculum levels? What training do you need?

B. ENGLISH

Standard 3 expects all teachers to promote high standards of literacy, articulacy and the correct use of standard English. Read through the following checklist of good practice.

- Pupils being *expected* to answer questions in developed phrases rather than just monosyllables, from Nursery onwards.

- Teachers giving time for pupils to develop fuller oral responses to questions posed.

- Teachers enabling pupils to pose questions to one another in order that pupils practise their sounds and speech patterns.

- Direct and regular intervention/correction from staff in *how* pupils speak and pronounce their letters.

- Staff (and governors) giving time to small groups of pupils in order to develop their conversation, vocabulary and basic social skills.

- The provision of structured and regular drama/acting opportunities in which pupils are expected to project their voice and practise speaking at length, with good eye contact.

- The use of music and rhyme to consolidate how young children are hearing and repeating sounds.

- The use of established EAL techniques (pattern, repetition, consolidation, elaboration) with pupils whose *first* language is English.

- The regular use of short dictations, across the curriculum, with an emphasis on keen listening and high-quality presentation of writing.

- A focus on how pupils are actually holding a pencil/pen and how they are forming their letters on a consistent basis.

- The regular use of limericks, couplets, verses, short poems being set to be learned by heart and for recitation in groups.

- Every opportunity taken by teachers and support staff to model and promote interesting vocabulary to match the age and needs of pupils.

REFLECTIONS AND EVIDENCE

1. Which of the above have you seen harnessed to good effect in classrooms you have observed? Are you building your own file of 'literacy/oracy top tips'?

2. How do you currently promote high standards of articulacy in your everyday teaching?

3. What approach do you (and your school) take to ensuring pupils use standard English correctly, orally and in writing?

4. Which of the above points could you integrate on a regular basis into your practice? How might you adapt any of them to best fit your particular subject area?

C. MATHEMATICS

Standard 3 expects primary teachers to have a clear understanding of appropriate teaching strategies for mathematics. Read the following checklist of good practice in maths lessons.

- Mathematical vocabulary clearly and creatively on display for pupils, with teachers and pupils referring regularly to this vocabulary.

- Pacy revision of number bonds and times tables, with divergent questioning from the teacher.

- Effective and consistent use of the school's calculation policy.

- Pupils making good use of learning scaffolds in the classroom, e.g. number lines, 100 squares, fraction grids, maths trays, Numicon, etc.

- Portable devices and use of IT to enhance mathematical learning.

- Maths 'challenge' and 'double challenge' tables containing suitable materials to extend more able mathematicians.

- A 'number of the week' display for oral and written responses: the answer is 28 – what is the question?

- Evidence of *applied* mathematics within and beyond the classroom walls.

REFLECTIONS AND EVIDENCE

- What very good practice with early years and primary maths have you observed and made notes on?

- Which of the above in your own practice have led pupils to make the quickest gains in their mathematical understanding?

- Which of the above have been most valuable to (a) the more able and (b) the less able mathematicians?

- What do you weave into each week's lesson plans to ensure there are opportunities for pupils to *apply* new maths knowledge beyond the classroom? Do you share your ideas with colleagues and learn from theirs?

D. INTELLECTUAL CURIOSITY

Standard 3 and **Standard 4** stipulate the teacher's responsibility to promote the value of scholarship, a love of learning and intellectual curiosity. Read the following and then reflect on your own practice.

Programmes of study and series of lessons which promote intellectual curiosity and scholarship enable pupils to:

- make sense of and deal creatively and positively with the circumstances of their lives, their current environment and the world at large;

- command language in its major forms and use them readily, competently and easily to serve their purposes;

- think creatively and purposefully in what might be described as the scientific mode – i.e. they observe critically, assemble evidence, analyse and reflect on what they have discovered, draw conclusions based on evidence and thoughts, test their conclusions as far as possible, adapt and restructure these according to the outcomes of testing, communicate their conclusions to others;

- learn to think, respond and behave according to the form and conventions of major disciplines, that is they are able, where necessary, to act as scientists, historians, geographers, technologists and mathematicians would;

- command essential learning skills, e.g. they are comfortable with and can use modern technology to suit their learning purposes;

- go on learning in a progressive way, building on what they have acquired and mastered, impelled by an abiding sense of curiosity;

- have a strong moral and ethical sense and the capacity to relate sympathetically with others;

- possess a critical faculty which enables them to distinguish between the substantial and the trivial, the genuine and the spurious, and to identify the crucial points in argument, data, literature and presentation.

REFLECTIONS AND EVIDENCE

1. In your own teaching (and it may well depend on the age range) which of the above do you think are the more important to promote among pupils?

2. Reflect on a very good lesson you have taught where you enabled pupils really *to become* scientists or historians or mathematicians? What was the cocktail of the lesson? What really enthused pupils?

3. What wider reading, viewing and independent study, perhaps linked to homework, do you set regularly for pupils to excite their intellectual curiosity?

4. How do you keep your own knowledge of subjects up-to-date and thus able to 'inspire, motivate and challenge pupils' (**Standard 1**)? Do you keep a record of your own wider reading, viewing and research?

E. DIFFERENTIATION

Standard 2 highlights the importance of teachers being fully aware of pupils' capabilities and prior knowledge, and planning lessons accordingly.

Standard 5 indicates that teachers must know when and how to differentiate appropriately. Experienced and new teachers alike are of one mind in saying that to provide creatively and consistently for a range of abilities in a class of 25 diverse pupils *is* demanding. Just about the hardest aspect of teaching any group remains getting 'the learning moments' right for individuals' different abilities and aptitudes.

Read through the following checklist of what skilful teachers do in well differentiated lessons.

- Know pupils' prior attainment and prior *knowledge* of a subject.
- Track meticulously pupils' progress in different *skills* within a subject.
- Think through which pupils work best with others.
- Judge the optimum size of a group for a particular activity.
- Judge when to intervene with impact and when to allow meaningful digressions.
- Gauge when independent learning will best deepen knowledge and understanding.
- Know when best to harness the library or iPad to expand pupils' thinking.
- Set meaningful homework within the lesson, well structured for individual needs.
- Know which factors inhibit progress and remove those barriers promptly.
- Practise 'differentiation down', pitching the lesson at the higher attainers and then providing suitable 'scaffolding' for other learners.

REFLECTIONS AND EVIDENCE

1. What records have you kept of lessons where you felt you were not successful in differentiation? What did you do differently the next time you taught the topic?

2. Reflect on a sequence of lessons where you know you succeeded with skilful differentiation. What techniques did you harness to capture the sustained engagement of pupils? What feedback did the pupils give you?

(Continued)

(Continued)

3. Which techniques from the checklist above have you found useful in your own classroom practice?

4. When you compare notes with other colleagues, are there similarities and differences in techniques for skilful differentiation depending on the subject matter being taught? Compare, for example, differentiation in science, geography, mathematics.

F. DEPLOYMENT OF TEACHING ASSISTANTS

Standard 8 expects all classroom teachers, where appropriate, to deploy support staff effectively. What does this mean in practice? The following checklist presents ways in which teaching and learning assistants can make a valuable contribution to and have an impact on pupils' learning and progress, with a particular focus on pupils with special educational needs.

*   Ensure pupils are ready to engage right at the start of a lesson with the correct equipment.

*   Help pupils understand lesson objectives and lesson outcomes.

*   Communicate assessment criteria so pupils understand what is required of them.

*   Discuss attainment and performance targets with pupils.

*   Empower pupils to work independently and show resilience when tasks are demanding.

*   Encourage positive collaborative work with their peers.

*   Enable pupils to self-assess and assess constructively the work of fellow pupils.

*   Provide guidance on interpreting and following up formative marking.

*   Adjust the pace and timing of activities to consolidate and deepen learning.

*   Reinforce the lesson plenary to set the scene for future learning.

*   Ensure homework tasks are accurately recorded.

*   Personalise praise and criticism linked to behaviour and achievement.

The Education Endowment Foundation (EEF, 2015) conducted a meta-analysis on the use of teaching assistants in the classroom and found that the number of TAs has more than trebled since 2000: from 79,000 to 243,700, while the number of teachers had remained fairly constant. A key finding was that *The typical deployment and use of TAs, under everyday conditions, is not leading to improvements in academic outcomes* (EEF, 2015, p7). Given the number of TAs and the cost of employing them, it is vital that they be deployed in the most effective way. The report, therefore, made some key recommendations. Given the size and status of the study, it is worth considering whether the suggested practice is evident in the schools you visit and work in:

1. TAs should not be used as an informal teaching resource for low-attaining pupils.

2. Use TAs to add value to what teachers do, not replace them.

3. Use TAs to help pupils develop independent learning skills and manage their own learning.

4. Ensure TAs are fully prepared for their role in the classroom.

5. Use TAs to deliver high quality one-to-one and small-group support using structured interventions.

6. Adopt evidence-based interventions to support TAs in their small-group and one-to-one instruction.

7. Ensure explicit connections are made between learning from everyday classroom teaching and structured interventions.

REFLECTIONS AND EVIDENCE

1. Which of the above features have you observed in other colleagues' classrooms? Which seemed to be of greatest value to pupils with special educational needs?

2. From your own experiences with other adults in your classroom, how have they been effective with any of the tasks above? What have support staff done which has accelerated the progress of pupils with whom they were working?

3. What have you found is the best preparation you can give to teaching assistants in order to maximise their impact on pupils' progress? What record-keeping is of value?

4. What problems, if any, have you experienced with managing other adults in your classroom? Have you shared concerns with your mentor to resolve difficulties which can and do occur?

14

SUCCESSFUL SCHOOLS, SUCCESSFUL TEACHERS

What is the cocktail of very good schools where teachers want to be, and which enjoy parental and student confidence, in the UK and globally?

All around the school there are places of interest, challenge, wonder and reflection. The student voice is listened to and acted upon. The staff are committed to excellent teaching and an orderly, enthusiastic community. The leadership of the school promotes an aspirational culture – one of belief that children and young people can achieve more than they might have thought. Governors, parents and local people hold the school in high regard, and are involved in productive discourse about its vision and performance.

In summary, certain aspects stand out from the norm, both to those who work in the school, and to visitors who observe: 'Someone's doing something special here.'

And it's all about execution. It is not enough to get the ideas right – they have to be adopted. It is not enough to adopt them – they have to be implemented correctly. And it is not enough to implement them correctly – they have to be constantly reviewed and adjusted over time as leaders see what works and what doesn't. The late Steve Jobs proclaimed a similar mantra at Apple, encouraging his workforce to 'fail wisely' in developing new products.

We are all deeply interested in doing better tomorrow what we did today. All the most successful schools I know are restless to get better. They simply aren't content to stand still. So what do they do?

FIVE STEPS

First, they interrogate current routines; they confront comfortable orthodoxies; they challenge why they do what they do, from minor practical details to major policies.

Second, they harness a wide range of carefully gathered data, qualitative and quantitative; they know what pupils, staff, parents, governors, the wider community identify as strengths and relative weaknesses.

Third, they respond with timely, small-scale innovation pinpointed on a clear aspect for development. Committed 'can do' innovators on the staff show that a hitherto intractable problem can be solved, thoughtfully, and at the right pace for the school community.

Fourth, the small-scale innovation wins the hearts and minds of others. Gradually, whole-scale innovation takes root. Experiences and outcomes for pupils and staff are enriched.

Fifth – and to complete the virtuous circle – the school has now moved to a higher operational level; it is in a position to interrogate its routines from a better place.

Restless schools are the ones that flourish. Reviewing and adjusting over time is the key to reinvigorating any business. Otherwise, stagnation beckons.

GOOD TO OUTSTANDING

Digging beneath the surface of the restless school questing for excellence, unsurprisingly you will find that there is a lot going on, though the staff may not be shouting about it – they are happily focused. What are these key features within the UK system, shaped significantly by the Ofsted inspection framework?

When schools receive a 'good' Ofsted inspection, they decide that to achieve 'outstanding' is a natural next step. Senior leaders ask all staff to read the reports of schools which have been judged 'outstanding'. Staff then commit themselves to ensuring that the same kind of phrases they have been reading in 'outstanding' reports can, in time, be readily written about their own school. Schools place great emphasis on everyone in the school knowing and understanding the language of the Ofsted framework. In-service sessions are focused on all teaching and support staff securing a strong grasp of the difference between Ofsted's 'good' and 'outstanding', whether in relation to teaching, pupils' learning behaviours or leadership at all levels.

Further, senior leaders in schools try to 'climb inside the inspector's skin'. Leaders seek to share with all staff how the inspection process works, with inspectors trained to focus on students' learning and progress rather than making judgements just about teaching.

Of course, confident leaders know that an Ofsted inspection is a passing event, albeit that its verdict is important to the school community. Day in and day out, the restless schools accept no substitute for an evidence-based approach to what is happening in classrooms. Senior staff are not able to engage in anecdotal talk about, say, the under-performing science coordinator or head of design and technology, because the senior team has clear and systematic evidence, rooted in regular lesson observations and teachers' own self-evaluations, on how all staff are performing in classrooms.

In these thriving contexts headteachers place great store by how well they create 'a sense of urgency at the right time' and a shared 'it's never too late' mentality among all staff. Headteachers recognise that not everything can be achieved at the same time, but that staff can 'shift gear' for a sustained period of time if there is that collective ambition to improve the school. Leaders at all levels believe that if change is worth introducing, why wait until a convenient point in the calendar, say the start of the following term? If pupils' experiences can be improved sooner, then the school should change its practices without delay. This is not a recipe for undue haste, but for accelerating change when change is required.

Equally, senior leaders and governors believe strongly in a 'no surprises' culture, and thus the importance of well embedded systems that alert staff if pupils are at risk of under-achieving and under-attaining. Complementing the finely-tuned organisational systems across the school is an open, trusting culture, one within which staff know that success is applauded and failure is supported rather than inviting blame.

In addition, leaders are very focused on eliminating 'in-school variation', or at least reaching a point where this has been reduced to an absolute minimum. One headteacher still striving for the school to be judged 'outstanding' made his mantra for the academic year: 'Let's all have a good year at the same time.'

Headteachers insist that communication of the highest quality, modelled by senior leaders, is at the heart of a high-performing institution. Such communication is always anticipating staff's and students' interests and concerns, so that the school is not side-tracked by rumour, gossip and unnecessary anxiety. There is an unequivocal sense that a 'we' not 'I' culture prevails. Leaders set out genuinely to see the best in people and dwell on the positive, while at the same time being single-minded in rooting out mediocrity.

TIGHTENING AND LOOSENING

There are, in my view, two final and telling characteristics of the successful, restless school.

First, the best schools 'tighten up' to be good, but 'loosen' to become outstanding. They recognise the importance of high levels of quality control to secure good provision, evolving into higher levels of quality assurance. Thus a whole-school culture of excellence is created, within which teachers and students alike feel empowered to take measured risks.

In the end, what are schools about if not what happens in classrooms? It is the accomplished, freed teacher, comfortable in her own knowledge of subject matter, who is able to master and manage high-quality digression. To watch creative intellectual digression which builds on pupils' previous knowledge and dares them to think differently – whether in the early years outdoor learning area or in an A level chemistry seminar – is to witness fine learning.

Second, the successful, restless school is fundamentally 'outward-facing'. Significant numbers of staff work on external agendas, sometimes linked to training school status, sometimes linked to federations and primary-secondary clusters. These schools enjoy partnerships with other schools and education providers: their staff are constantly bringing back good ideas into their own classrooms from external sources.

And a key aspect of this outward-facing philosophy is the way in which the schools cite the value of 'external critical friends' who are invited from time to time to see the school 'with a fresh pair of eyes'. These friends validate changes, champion great practice and point out where there is still scope for development.

Successful schools and their leaders are restless. There is a strange paradox at their core: they are very secure in their systems, values and successes yet simultaneously seek to change and improve. These schools look inwards to secure wise development; they look outwards to seize innovation which they can shape to their own ends and, importantly, make a difference to the children and students they serve.

REFLECTIONS

1. From your experiences of schools which you have visited and taught in, what do you think makes up the cocktail of very good schools?

2. What good practice have you seen with schools (departments, faculties, sections, teams) keeping themselves under constant review which leads to improvements?

3. What in your view makes for effective leadership, at all levels, in schools?

4. What are the merits of the argument outlined above about 'outward-facing' schools?

5. What do you understand, in the context of both schools and individual classrooms, about the notion of 'tightening and loosening'?

6. What steps are you taking to prepare yourself for a leadership position ahead, either in your current school or another? What support are you receiving from a mentor or senior member of staff in such preparation?

APPENDIX

TEACHERS' STANDARDS POSTERS

(Posters issued to schools in 2012 by the DfE)

TEACHERS' STANDARDS

Myths and facts

Myth: Schools can keep their existing Performance Management policies because the new Appraisal Regulations are permissive and do not require anything new.
Fact: Although in general the new Appraisal Regulations allow schools much more flexibility than the 2006 Performance Management regulations, they have introduced one new requirement. In future, teachers' performance must be assessed against the Teachers' Standards. Appraisal policies that do not provide for assessment of performance against the Teachers' Standards will not comply with the 2012 Appraisal Regulations.
Myth: The Teachers' Standards apply only to teachers in maintained schools.
Fact: Academies and independent schools will not have to assess their teachers' performance against Part One of the Teachers' Standards as part of an annual appraisal process. If they take part in statutory induction arrangements, they will, however, have to assess NQTs against the Standards at the end of their induction period.

(Continued)

(Continued)

Part Two of the Teachers' Standards applies to all teachers , including those in academies and independent schools.
Myth: Headteachers and other members of the Leadership group should not be assessed against the Teachers' Standards.
Fact: Headteachers, deputies and assistant heads are covered by the Appraisal Regulations and also need to be assessed against the Teachers' Standards. Appraisers should use their common sense when assessing performance against the Standards.
Myth: Post-Threshold, Excellent Teachers and ASTs should not be assessed against the Teachers' Standards.
Fact: As part of the annual appraisal process, the performance of post-Threshold, ETs and ASTs in maintained schools must be assessed against the Teachers' Standards. Schools can, if they wish, also assess these teachers against relevant higher standards.   In addition, any teacher applying for assessment against higher standards will first be assessed against the Teachers' Standards.
Myth: The Teachers' Standards cannot be used to assess the performance of QTLS teachers.
Fact: It is up to schools to decide which standards they wish to use when assessing the performance of QTLS teachers. There is no requirement for schools to assess QTLS teachers' performance against the Teachers' Standards , but they can do so if they wish.
Myth: There are three new Career Stages for teachers: 'NOT', 'mid-career teachers' and 'more experienced practitioners'.
Fact: These are not rigid career stages but examples of different levels of experience that teachers might have. Teachers' performance should be assessed against the Teachers' Standards to a level that is consistent with what should reasonably be expected of a teacher, given their current role and their level of experience. Schools will naturally have higher expectations of their experienced teachers than they will of their NOTs.
Myth: Schools should adopt a model which exemplifies the Teachers' Standards for teachers at different levels of experience.
Fact: The independent review group considered and rejected the suggestion that expectations should be defined for teachers at different career stages.   The government agrees that it is not necessary or helpful for schools to adopt rigid models that seek to set out exactly what the Teachers' Standards mean for teachers at different points on the pay scale. Headteachers and others should use their professional judgement and common sense when appraising teachers' performance against the Teachers' Standards.
Myth: The Threshold, Advanced Skills and Excellent Teacher pay grades are being abolished and replaced with Master Teachers.
Fact: The Teachers' Standards Review Group recommended in its second report that the existing standards for Post-Threshold, Excellent Teacher and Advanced Skills Teacher should be discontinued, and that a new Master Teacher Standard should be introduced.

The Secretary of State welcomed this recommendation in principle, but the School Teachers' Review Body will need to advise on the future of these existing pay grades. No decision has yet been taken and the current post-Threshold, ET and AST standards will continue as they are for the time being.

Myth: Teachers' performance will be assessed against the Teachers' Standards from 1 September 2012.

Fact: Although the Appraisal Regulations come into force on 1 September 2012, most teachers' next appraisals are likely to take place under the 2006 performance management regulations, because those regulations continue to apply in relation to any performance management cycle already in progress on 1 September 2012.

From September 2012, any teacher applying for assessment against higher standards will first be assessed against the Teachers' Standards.

The Teachers' Standards can be found on the DfE website: **www.education.gov.uk/ publications**.

How will they be used?

A relentless focus on high-quality teachers and teaching requires a clear and universal understanding of the basic elements of good teaching. The standards which define our expectations for teachers' professional practice should therefore set the benchmark for excellent teaching and exemplary personal conduct. They should set a standard to which all trainees aspire, and which all qualified teachers adhere to and improve upon throughout the various stages of their career.

Sally Coates, Chair of the independent Teachers' Standards Review and Principal of Burlington Danes Academy.

What are the Teachers' Standards?

- The Teachers' Standards set a clear baseline of expectations for the professional practice and conduct of teachers and define the minimum level of practice expected of all teachers in England.
- They were developed by an independent review group made up of leading teachers, head-teachers and other experts.

Practising teachers will use the Teachers' Standards to support their own professional development and growth.

- They can be used by individual teachers to review their practice and inform their plans for continuing professional development.
- The most successful education systems in the world are characterised by high levels of lesson observation. Teachers benefit from observing each others' practice in the classroom. Teachers learn best from other professionals. Observing teaching and being observed and having the opportunity to plan, prepare, reflect and teach with other teachers can help to improve the quality of teaching.
- Many teachers are keen to improve their own practice by having feedback on their own practice from colleagues and from observing the practice of others.

(Continued)

(Continued)

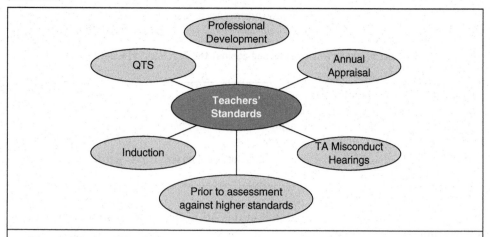

> The new Teachers' Standards give an unequivocal message that highly effective teaching is what matters in this profession.
>
> The Review Group has seized the opportunity to raise the bar for current and future teachers. Our nation's children and young people deserve no less.
>
> > Roy Blatchford, Deputy Chair of the independent Teachers' Standards Review and Director of the National Education Trust.

Those involved in training and inducting new teachers will use the Teachers' Standards to ensure quality of new entrants to the profession.

- The Teachers' Standards will be used by Initial Teacher Training (ITT) providers to assess when trainees can be recommended for Qualified Teacher Status.
- They will be used by schools to assess the extent to which Newly Qualified Teachers can demonstrate their competence at the end of their Induction period.

Headteachers and other school leaders will use the Teachers' Standards to improve teachers' quality by setting minimum expectations of teaching in their schools.

- The Teachers' Standards will be used by maintained schools to assess teachers' performance and help schools and teachers to identify development needs and plan professional development.
- Headteachers (or other appraisers) are expected to assess teachers to a level that is consistent with what should reasonably be expected of a teacher given their role and their level of experience.
- They will also be used to ensure that teachers meet minimum standards if they apply for assessment against higher standards (post-Threshold, AST and ET).

The Teaching Agency will use the Teachers' Standards when hearing cases of serious misconduct.

- Since April 2012, Part Two of the Teachers' Standards can be used by the Teaching Agency when hearing cases of serious misconduct, regardless of the setting where a teacher works.

> [The Teachers' Standards] set clear expectations about the skills that every teacher in our schools should demonstrate. They will make a significant improvement to teaching by ensuring teachers can focus on the skills that matter most.
>
> > Michael Gove, Secretary of State for Education launching the Teachers' Standards in July 2011.

The Teachers' Standards can be found on the DfE website: **www.education.gov.uk/ publications**.

Teachers' Standards

PREAMBLE
Teachers make the education of their pupils their first concern and are accountable for achieving the highest possible standards in work and conduct. Teachers act with honesty and integrity, have strong subject knowledge, keep their knowledge and skills as teachers up to date and are self-critical, forge positive professional relationships and work with parents in the best interests of their pupils.
PART ONE: TEACHING
A teacher must :
1 Set high expectations which inspire, motivate and challenge pupils
• establish a safe and stimulating environment for pupils, rooted in mutual respect • set goals that stretch and challenge pupils of all backgrounds, abilities and dispositions • demonstrate consistently the positive attitudes, values and behaviour which are expected of pupils.
2 Promote good progress and outcomes by pupils
• be accountable for pupils' attainment, progress and outcomes • be aware of pupils' capabilities and their prior knowledge, and plan teaching to build on these • guide pupils to reflect on the progress they have made and their emerging needs • demonstrate knowledge and understanding of how pupils learn and how this impacts on teaching • encourage pupils to take a responsible and conscientious attitude to their own work and study.
3 Demonstrate good subject and curriculum knowledge
• have a secure knowledge of the relevant subject(s) and curriculum areas, foster and maintain pupils' interest in the subject and address misunderstandings • demonstrate a critical understanding of developments in the subject and curriculum areas and promote the value of scholarship • demonstrate an understanding of and take responsibility for promoting high standards of literacy, articulacy and the correct use of standard English, whatever the teacher's specialist subject • if teaching early reading, demonstrate a clear understanding of systematic synthetic phonics • if teaching early mathematics, demonstrate a clear understanding of appropriate teaching strategies.

(Continued)

(Continued)

---

4 Plan and teach well structured lessons

- impart knowledge and develop understanding through effective use of lesson time

- promote a love of learning and children's intellectual curiosity

- set homework and plan other out-of-class activities to consolidate and extend the knowledge and understanding pupils have acquired

- reflect systematically on the effectiveness of lessons and approaches to teaching

- contribute to the design and provision of an engaging curriculum within the relevant subject area(s).

5 Adapt teaching to respond to the strengths and needs of all pupils

- know when and how to differentiate appropriately, using approaches which enable pupils to be taught effectively

- have a secure understanding of how a range of factors can inhibit pupils' ability to learn and how best to overcome these

- demonstrate an awareness of the physical, social and intellectual development of children and know how to adapt teaching to support pupils' education at different stages of development

- have a clear understanding of the needs of all pupils, including those with special educational needs, those of high ability, those with English as an additional language and those with disabilities, and be able to use and evaluate distinctive teaching approaches to engage and support them.

6 Make accurate and productive use of assessment

- know and understand how to assess the relevant subject and curriculum areas, including statutory assessment requirements

- make use of formative and summative assessment to secure pupils' progress

- use relevant data to monitor progress, set targets and plan subsequent lessons

- give pupils regular feedback, both orally and through accurate marking, and encourage pupils to respond to the feedback.

7 Manage behaviour effectively to ensure a good and safe learning environment

- have clear rules and routines for behaviour in classrooms, and take responsibility for promoting good and courteous behaviour both in classrooms and around the school, in accordance with the school's behaviour policy

- have high expectations of behaviour and establish a framework for discipline with a range of strategies, using praise, sanctions and rewards consistently and fairly

- manage classes effectively, using approaches which are appropriate to pupils' needs in order to involve and motivate them

- maintain good relationships with pupils, exercise appropriate authority and act decisively when necessary.

8 Fulfil wider professional responsibilities

- make a positive contribution to the wider life and ethos of the school

- develop effective professional relationships with colleagues, knowing how and when to draw on advice and specialist support

- deploy support staff effectively

- take responsibility for improving teaching through appropriate professional development, responding to advice and feedback from colleagues

- communicate effectively with parents with regard to pupils' achievements and well-being.

PART TWO: PERSONAL AND PROFESSIONAL CONDUCT

A teacher is expected to demonstrate consistently high standards of personal and professional conduct. The following statements define the behaviour and attitudes which set the required standard for conduct throughout a teacher's career.

- Teachers uphold public trust in the profession and maintain high standards of ethics and behaviour, within and outside school, by :

  o treating pupils with dignity, building relationships rooted in mutual respect, and at all times observing proper boundaries appropriate to a teacher's professional position

  o having regard for the need to safeguard pupils' well-being, in accordance with statutory provisions

  o showing tolerance of and respect for the rights of others

  o not undermining fundamental British values, including democracy, the rule of law, individual liberty and mutual respect, and tolerance of those with different faiths and beliefs

  o ensuring that personal beliefs are not expressed in ways which exploit pupils' vulnerability or might lead them to break the law.

- Teachers must have proper and professional regard for the ethos, policies and practices of the school in which they teach, and maintain high standards in their own attendance and punctuality.

- Teachers must have an understanding of, and always act within, the statutory frameworks which set out their professional duties and responsibilities.

The Teachers' Standards can be found on the DfE website: **www.education.gov.uk/publications**.

RECOMMENDED BOOKS ON SCHOOLS AND TEACHING

Adcock, J (1994) *In Place of Schools*. London: New Education Press.

A radical, short volume on how schools will no longer exist by the mid-twenty-first century. The book challenges our ideas of what 'classrooms of the future' might look like.

Barber, M (1996) *The Learning Game: Arguments for an Education Revolution*. London: Gollancz.

This book shaped Prime Minister Tony Blair's 'Education Education Education' agenda – written by its chief architect.

Benn, M (2011) *School Wars*. London: Verso.

One of the most readable accounts of what is happening in education today with the coming of the Academy and Free School movement. The author believes strongly that the comprehensive school ideal is being lost.

Benson, AC (1902) *The Schoolmaster.* New York and London: G. Putnam's Sons.

Written by a master at Eton at the start of the twentieth century, what it has to say about the classroom is as true today as it was then: pupils don't change!

Blatchford, R (2014) *The Restless School*. Woodbridge, Suffolk: John Catt.

The author's exploration of the cocktail of high-performing classrooms and great schools, and how 'excellence as standard' will drive global school systems in the future.

Carr, JL (2003) *The Harpole Report*. Bury St Edmunds: Quince Tree Press.

A fictional, amusing history of a primary school, seen through the eyes of the beleaguered acting headteacher. Lots of delightful episodes, ideal for reading in assembly.

Chubb, JE and Moe, TM (1990) *Politics, Markets and America's Schools*. Washington, DC: Brookings Institution Press.

A provocative, seminal work which threw down the gauntlet to governments in America and beyond: should the state provide education or should it be left to the market?

Dunford, J (1998) *Her Majesty's Inspectorate of Schools since 1944*. London: Woburn Press.

Inspection has played a vital part in how schools and teaching have developed. John Dunford records this with wit and an eye for the right historical detail.

Gardner, H (2008) *Five Minds for the Future*. Boston, MA: Harvard Business School Press.

Much known for his work on multiple intelligences, Gardner defines here what he believes to be the essential kinds of minds required for twentieth-century teachers and pupils.

Glazzard, J (2016) *Learning to Be a Superhero [crossed out] Primary Teacher: Core Knowledge and Understanding*. Northwich: Critical Publishing.

An excellent, practical book with theoretical underpinnings, which is closely linked to the Teachers' Standards.

Hargreaves, D (1982) *The Challenge for the Comprehensive School*. London: Routledge & Kegan Paul.

For those interested in the evolution of the comprehensive school in this country, this is a must-read, beautifully written with plenty of anecdote.

Jolliffe, W and Waugh, D (2017) *The Beginning Teacher: A Guide to Developing Outstanding Practice*. London: Sage.

An edited book which provides guidance on a range of aspects of teaching, both primary and secondary, from experts in a range of fields.

Jolliffe, W, Waugh, D and Beverton, S with Stead, J (2014) *Supporting Secondary Readers*. London: Sage.

This book provides guidance for secondary teachers on developing students' literacy skills. It emphasises that every teacher is a teacher of reading.

McCourt, F (2005) *Teacher Man*. New York: Scribner.

A brilliant account of teaching in New York classrooms, full of urban myths, pathos and humour.

McKinsey & Co. (2007) *How the World's Best-performing School Systems Come Out on Top*. Available at: **www.mckinsey.com**.

A much-quoted text identifying the key characteristics of school systems globally which are performing very well today. The book has some telling observations on the vital importance of great teachers.

Phinn, G (1996) *Classroom Creatures*. Doncaster: Roselea Publications.

A collection of short poems – ideal for reading aloud in class – which capture the fun and fundamentals of classroom practice.

Robinson, S (2012) *School and School System Leadership*. London: Continuum.

An excellent and authoritative account of school leadership over the past two decades, and what this has meant for headteachers and teachers.

Smith, J (2000) *The Learning Game*. London: Little, Brown.

Written by a life-long teacher, in common with AC Benson's book above, there are not many teacher autobiographies that better this one. Short and highly readable.

Willingham, D (2009) *Why Don't Students Like School?* San Francisco: Jossey-Bass.

The book (by an American writer) poses a series of challenging questions about why pupils may not succeed at school and seeks to present some answers, some not altogether orthodox.

Winkley, D (2002) *Handsworth Revolution*. London: Giles de la Mare Publishers.

One headteacher's true account of transforming a large inner-city primary school, set against political and social events of the latter part of the twentieth century.

REFERENCES

Archer, L, Dawson, E, DeWitt, J, Seakins, A and Wong, B (2015) Science capital: a conceptual, methodological, and empirical argument for extending Bourdieusian notions of capital beyond the arts. *Journal of Research in Science Teaching*, 52, 7, pp922–48.

Clark, JM and Paivio, A (1991) Dual coding theory and education, in Educational Psychology Review, 3, pp149–210. Cited in Ofsted (2019b) Education Inspection Framework: Overview of Research. Available at: **www.ofsted.gov.uk**.

Department for Education (2011a) First Report of the Independent Review of Teachers' Standards: OTS and Core Standards. London: DfE. Available at: **www.education.gov.uk**.

Department for Education (2011b) Second Report of the Independent Review of Teachers' Standards: Post-threshold, Excellent Teacher and Advanced Skills Teacher Standards. London: DfE. Available at: **www.education.gov.uk**.

Department for Education (2012a) *Teachers' Standards*. London: DfE. Available at: **www.education.gov.uk**.

Department for Education (2012b) *School Teachers' Pay and Conditions Document 2012*. London: DfE. Available at **www.education.gov.uk**.

Department for Education (2013) *The National Curriculum in England*. London: DfE. Available at: **www.education.gov.uk**.

Education Endowment Foundation (2015) *Making Best Use of Teaching Assistants*, Guidance Report (produced by Jonathan Sharples, Rob Webster, Peter Blatchford). London: EEF. Available at **https://v1.educationendowmentfoundation.org.uk/uploads/pdf/TA_Guidance_Report_Interactive.pdf** (accessed 24 April 2017).

General Medical Council (2012) *Good Medical Practice*. Available at **www.gmc-uk.org**.

Ofsted (2019a) *School Inspection Handbook*. London: Ofsted. Available at **www.ofsted.gov.uk**.

Ofsted (2019b) *Education Inspection Framework: Overview of Research.* Available at: **www.ofsted.gov.uk**.

Ofsted (2020a) *The Annual Report of Her Majesty's Chief Inspector of Education, Children's Services and Skills.* London. Ofsted. Available at **www.ofsted.gov.uk**.

Ofsted (2020b) Amanda Spielman launches Ofsted's Annual Report 2018/19. Transcript of speech. Available at **www.ofsted.gov.uk**.

Paivio, A (1990) *Mental Representations: A Dual Coding Approach.* Oxford University Press. Cited in Ofsted (2019b) *Education Inspection Framework: Overview of Research.* Available at: **www.ofsted.gov.uk**.

Rawson, KA and Kintsch, W (2005) Rereading effects depend on time of test. *Journal of Educational Psychology,* 97, 1, pp70–80. Cited in Ofsted (2019b) *Education Inspection Framework: Overview of Research.* Available at: **www.ofsted.gov.uk**.

Rohrer, D (2012) Interleaving helps students distinguish among similar concepts. *Educational Psychology Review,* 24, pp355–67. Cited in Ofsted (2019b) *Education Inspection Framework: Overview of Research.* Available at: **www.ofsted.gov.uk**.

Rutter, M, Maughan, B, Mortimore, P and Ouston, J with Smith, A (1979) *Fifteen Thousand Hours: Secondary Schools and Their Effects on Children.* London: Open Books.

INDEX